RELIGION IN THE AGE OF EXPLORATION: THE CASE OF SPAIN AND NEW SPAIN

Proceedings
of the Fifth Annual Symposium
of the Philip M. and Ethel Klutznick
Chair in Jewish Civilization
October 25 & 26, 1992

Studies in Jewish Civilization—5

RELIGION IN THE AGE OF EXPLORATION: THE CASE OF SPAIN AND NEW SPAIN

Bryan F. Le Beau
Menachem Mor
Editors

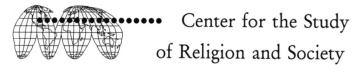 Center for the Study
of Religion and Society
The Klutznick Chair in Jewish Civilization

Creighton University Press

ISBN: 1-881871-21-5
ISSN: 1070-8510
LC Catalog Card: 95-083916

Editorial:
Creighton University Press
2500 California Plaza
Omaha, Nebraska 68178

Marketing and Distribution:
Fordham University Press
University Box L
Bronx, New York 10458

Printed in the United States of America

In Memory
Janice Friedman Yale
1948 — 1995

Contents

Acknowledgments

Most of the papers in this collection were delivered at the Fifth Annual Symposium of the Philip M. and Ethel Klutznick Chair in Jewish Civilization at Creighton University on October 25 and 26, 1992.

We would like to thank the many people involved in the preparation of the symposium. Special thanks to Beth Seldin Dotan, director of the Jewish Cultural Arts Council from 1989-1994, who was so instrumental in making the Sunday events a success; to the College of Jewish Learning, a group with a deep commitment to Jewish education under the leadership of Steve Riekes; to the Jewish Federation of Omaha for their unstinting support; to Caryn Rifkin on her fifth annual "tour of duty" with the Symposium; and to Maryellen Read for coordinating the event and for her careful preparation of the entire collection of papers.

We wish to thank the following for the financial contributions which funded this symposium:

Creighton College of Arts and Sciences
The Jewish Cultural Arts Council
The Henry Monsky Lodge of B'nai B'rith
Lawrence I. Batt
The Ike and Roz Friedman Foundation
The Jewish Memorial Foundation for Jewish Culture
A.A. and Ethel Yossem Endowment Fund

Bryan F. Le Beau, Director
Center for the Study of
Religion and Society
Creighton University
Omaha, Nebraska

Menachem Mor, Chairman
Department of Jewish History
University of Haifa
Haifa, Israel
December, 1995

Editors' Introduction

As the title suggests, the papers in this collection address various topics related to religion in the Age of Exploration, or from the fifteenth through the eighteenth centuries. They are focused principally on Spain and New Spain, with particular, but not exclusive, attention paid to the history of Jews in those areas. Seven of the papers were delivered on October 25-26, 1992, on the Quincentennial of the Columbian Encounter at the Fifth Annual Klutznick Symposium. The symposium was co-hosted by Creighton University's Philip M. and Ethel Klutznick Chair in Jewish Civilization and Center for the Study of Religion and Society. Two papers have been added in order to lend further substance to the collection.

The first three papers deal with Jews in fifteenth century Spain. As Rochelle Millen writes, the Spanish expulsion of the Jews in 1492 marked the end of a period of cultural richness among Jews of the Iberian peninsula. In the first paper included herein, she discusses the contributions to that cultural Renaissance of Isaac Abravanel. Millen analyzes Abravanel's concept of monarchy. She shows how Abravanel dealt with the question of the best form of human government. She presents a fifteenth century Renaissance man par excellence whose ideas were nevertheless in part medieval, a man of reason who was an anti-rationalist as well. Abravanel's notion of monarchy, Millen argues, was an integral part both of his understanding of the people of Israel and of the purpose of Torah. His writings, she concludes, directly influenced the mystical messianism which pervaded Jewish intellectual life in the 200 years after his death.

A subject of considerable interest to historians of Spain in the pre-expulsion period is the forced conversion of Jews. In 1391 tens of thousands of Jews in Spain were forcibly baptized and converted to Catholicism. Ninety years later the Spanish Inquisition charged many of those converts who continued to practice Judaism, called judaizers, with heresy. In "Judaizing Women in Castile," one of the two papers added to those presented at the 1992 symposium, Renée Levine

Melammed draws upon Inquisition documents and detailed records from the trials that resulted to describe the uneasy lives of one group of women judaizers, those of Castile. The element of continuity in the midst of a vanishing Jewish community, Melammed argues, is the most remarkable aspect of their lives. In the face of great adversity their continued persistence in transmitting knowledge of their heritage assured the survival of judaizing even after the Expulsion.

In the second paper added to the collection for publication, Lewis Tambs addresses the watershed event of Jewish history in the Age of Exploration, the expulsion of the Jews from Spain. Tambs provides a brief history of the Jewish community in Spain. He discusses the relationship between Jews and Christians and Muslims, as well as the impact on Spanish Jews of the Reconquest and Spanish Inquisition, thus setting the stage for the expulsion of 1492. Tambs points to the many motives that contributed to Ferdinand and Isabella's decision to issue the Edict of Expulsion, including religious fervor, desire to defend the Faith against apostasy and heresy, determination to unite Spain under one religious tradition, fear of the Jews as a Fifth Column in the face of the Moorish menace, *converso* animosity toward their former co-religionists, Genoese commercial competition, and the Crown's greed for Jewish gold. In the end, however, he sees it as nothing less that an act of injustice.

The other watershed event of 1492, of course, was the voyage of Christopher Columbus to what was for Europeans a new world. The result was not only a biological and cultural exchange, but also a religious encounter that changed the course of history. In the first of two papers on Columbus, Hector Avalos provides insight into that encounter by demonstrating the eschatological framework for Columbus' voyage and views of the world he "discovered." In an attempt to bring to light a side of Columbus' character seldom considered in recent studies, "Columbus as biblical exegete," Avalos shows that years before his fateful journey Columbus began to record biblical passages that he believed supported that part of his Enterprise of the Indies which called for a search for long-lost biblical lands.

Avalos surveys Columbus' selection of biblical passages and use of exegetical techniques in his *Libro de las profeciás*. He argues that, although Columbus believed in the prophecies his research revealed, he originally intended his collection to serve as a compendium for his propaganda, whereby he would win Crown support for his voyage. Further, as he made his most substantive compilations after his enterprise had been vindicated in 1492, Avalos concludes, Columbus ultimately intended *Libro* to provide the substance for a yet to be composed glorious epic of his voyage and accomplishments.

Jonathan Sarna's "The Mythical Jewish Columbus and the History of America's Jews," the symposium's keynote address, explores some myths connecting Jews to America's founding. In 1894 Meyer (Moritz) Kayserling wrote *Christopher Columbus and the Participation of the Jews in the Spanish and Portuguese Discoveries,* the most significant American Jewish contribution to the celebration of the 400th anniversary of Columbus' landing in the New World. The book validated American Jewry's sense that it had deep roots in America, Sarna writes, that it had contributed substantially to the nation's development, and that as a result it deserved respect. The idea that Columbus himself might have been a Jew, however, arose in non-Jewish circles in Spain. Its popularity peaked during the 1930s, when the "Jewish question" was very much on people's minds. Although based almost entirely on circumstantial evidence and rejected by most Jewish scholars, the idea won considerable popular adherence, Sarna offers, because Jews believed it would gain them greater national respect.

"The other side of the story" of religion in the Age of Exploration, to use Dale Stover's words, tells of the arrival of Christianity in the Americas and of the indigenous response to that arrival. *Religion in the Age of Exploration* includes two papers on the subject. In the first, while presenting the distinctive views of indigenous Americans, Stover demonstrates the complexity—as opposed to the popularly perceived uniformity—of the Native American interpretation of Christian beliefs. He corrects certain European misconstructions of the religious existence of the indigenous peoples of the "New World" and provides a critical indigenous perspective on the European mind-set which underlay that misconstruction and that has influenced Euroamerican identity and Euroamerican-Native American relations to the present.

Gordon Bronitsky provides a case-in-point from the history of Spanish Catholic evangelization of Native Americans. He discusses Spanish missionization among the indigenous people of New Mexico in the seventeenth century; the Pueblo Revolt of 1680 and its relationship to missionization; the consequences of the Reconquest of New Mexico in 1693 on Native religions; Catholic evangelization during the Mexican period; and the interplay among Catholic, Protestant, and Native religions during the American period (post-1848). Bronitsky argues that despite the efforts of Spanish missions true conversion of Native Americans never occurred. Instead, they adopted a strategy of religious accommodation sometimes referred to as compartmentalization.

The encounter between Europeans and Native Americans affected the course of religious thinking among Europeans and Euro-Americans as well. Gershon Greenberg provides examples of that effect in "American Indians, Lost Tribes and Christian Eschatology." The American Indian—Ten Lost Tribes connection has long been regarded as just an interesting fantasy. Greenberg, however, demonstrates how it was once used by serious scholars for purposes of Protestant understanding and developing the Mormon religion. He shows how the connection was used to validate the view that America was to be the staging ground for the Christian *eschaton*. The Lost Tribes, now found, Greenberg explains, completed the discovery of dispersed Jews which was to herald the millennium. As part of this drama, American Indians were to convert to Christianity and abandon American soil to American Protestants for the redeemed Jerusalem in the Land of Israel.

And, finally, Yitzchak Kerem returns us to the subject of Jews in the Age of Exploration, this time in seventeenth and eighteenth century North America. In particular, Kerem discusses the religious conflict between Sephardic settlers—the descendants of Jews expelled from Spain and Portugal—in the Dutch- and English-speaking areas of North America. To Jewish settlers the colonies symbolized a future of freedom where their religious practices and communal life could flourish, as well as a land and people into which they could integrate and to the development of which they could contribute. Legislation enacted in opposition to the inclusion of Jews during the Colonial Period and even after the establishment of the United States, however, threatened to thwart that dream. Kerem shows how Jews overcame such obstacles by finding avenues by which to exert political influence, enter the political arena, and hold public office.

Attention paid to religion in the Age of Exploration has not been limited to the 1992 Columbian Quincentennial. It has fascinated historians for decades, if not centuries, and resulted in publications that now fill library shelves. Nevertheless, the entire story has not been told. *Religion in the Age of Exploration* is another contribution to the telling of that story.

List of Contributors

Hector Avalos

Department of Religious Studies
and Latino Studies Program
Iowa State University
403 Ross Hall
Ames, Iowa 50011-2063

Gordon Bronitsky

Bronitsky and Associates
3551 South Monaco Parkway
Suite 195
Denver, Colorado 80237

Gershon Greenberg

Department of Philosophy and Religion
The American University
4400 Massachusetts Ave., N.W.
Washington, D.C. 20016-8056

Yitzchak Kerem

Department of Modern Greek History
Aristotle University
Thessaloniki, Greece

Bryan F. Le Beau

Center for the Study of Religion
and Society
Creighton University
Omaha, Nebraska 68178

Renée Levine Melammed

The National Jewish Center
for Learning and Leadership
99 Park Ave., Suite C-300
New York, New York 10016-1599

Rochelle L. Millen   Department of Religion
                            Wittenberg University
                            Post Office Box 720
                            Springfield, Ohio 45501-0720

Menachem Mor   Department of Jewish History
                            University of Haifa
                            Haifa, Israel 31999

Jonathan Sarna   Department of Near Eastern Studies
                            Brandeis University
                            415 South St.
                            Waltham, Massachusetts 02254

Dale Stover   Department of Philosophy and Religion
                            University of Nebraska at Omaha
                            Omaha, Nebraska 68182-0265

Lewis A. Tambs   Department of History
                            Arizona State University
                            Tempe, Arizona 85287-2501

Abravanel's Concept of Monarchy

Rochelle L. Millen

Historians sometimes date the beginning of the Renaissance with the art of Giotto, the early fourteenth century Florentine painter, sculptor and architect, or with the literary works of Petrarch. Certainly, by the time of the deaths of Giotto and Petrarch in the 1370s, Europe had actively stirred from its medieval slumber, and humanism, in its many forms, was developing at a rapid pace. Yet while Europe lumbered forward from the Dark Ages toward the light of Renaissance classicism and humanism, the fate of its Jewish community was otherwise.[1] One of the last flourishing Jewish communities on European soil—and the most populous[2]—was expelled from Spain in 1492. The Spanish expulsion is a watershed in Jewish history. It marks the end of a period of great cultural richness and diversity among the Jews of the Iberian peninsula—indeed a renaissance—and the beginning of three hundred years of medievalism. Thus, while Europe as a whole moved toward the flowering of art, literature and classical learning as the transition to the modern world, the Jews of Europe became increasingly cut off from the centers of western culture. The late medieval period of European Jewish history may be said to have spanned 1492 to 1789, from the Spanish expulsion until the French Revolution.

The life and writings of Don Isaac Abravanel, 1437-1508, manifest this unusual pattern. Abravanel was a Renaissance man, a humanist *par excellence.* He was versed not only in Hebrew and Portuguese, but also in Castilian and Latin; he studied not only Hebrew Bible and Talmud, but also the texts of medieval Jewish and Christian philosophy; he was familiar with Greek and Islamic philosophy, as well as the natural sciences of the time. The diversity of his political and intellectual accomplishments place him squarely in the Renaissance mode. Yet the

1

substance of Abravanel's writings indicate characteristics that may accurately be described as medieval.[3] He was active, yet his ideology advocated passivity.[4] He was a man of reason, but an anti- rationalist. Abravanel was worldly, yet strongly influenced the mystical messianism which pervaded Jewish intellectual life in the two hundred years after his death. The inner contradiction of partaking of the *Weltanschaung* of both the Renaissance and the Middle Ages is exemplified by Abravanel's writings on monarchy. Abravanel deals with the issue of monarchy—indeed with the broader question of the best form of human government—in his commentaries on both Deuteronomy 17:14f and I Samuel 8:6f. The former seems to command Israel to institute a king, while the latter describes the episode in which the Israelites ask Samuel for a king and both Samuel and God are offended. The political question for Abravanel thus arises as an exegetical issue: how are the two sets of verses to be reconciled?[5]

This paper will analyze Abravanel's attempt to resolve the apparent exegetical contradiction, trace the sources of the political theory put forth in the process, and conclude with an analytic summary of Abravanel's view of monarchy.

Abravanel begins by demonstrating that the earlier efforts to solve the seeming textual discrepancy are all based on the presupposition that Deuteronomy 17:14f expresses a divine command to establish a monarchy. Nahmanides, for instance, insists that the establishment of the king is a positive commandment, a matter of obligation, not choice.[6] The underlying conceptual presupposition of both the Christian and Jewish commentators espousing this view is that monarchy constitutes a superior—if not the best— form of human government. The commentators assume, Abravanel reasons, that God would prescribe for God's "holy nation" (Exodus 19:6) a political structure that is of the highest excellence and is therefore preferred to all others. Abravanel's analysis of these claims has two steps: to examine whether monarchy is indeed a preferred political structure, and to determine whether Deuteronomy 17:14f clearly means that Israel is obligated to establish it.

In regard to the first step, Abravanel asserts that philosophers[7] validate the necessity of monarchy by insisting that the three main requirements of a smoothly functioning government are best satisfied only in a monarchy. These are unity, continuity, and absolute power. Abravanel, however, insists that unity may be best attained through the consent of several rulers (implying, perhaps, an inclination toward oligarchy, republicanism, or theocracy). Abravanel seems to prefer a change of government, answerable to its constituency,[8] to the more likely corruptible rule of one king. The third condition, absolute power, is strongly opposed by Abravanel as a *sine qua non* of good government; it is not crucial nor even desirable. Rather, Abravanel insists that the power of the rulers be limited by the law. This definition of kingship—rule according to law—was fundamental to medieval political notions. But since the king's power was limited by law, wherein lies the danger of monarchy? The risk resides precisely in the attributes under consideration, *viz.* unity, continuity and absolute power. For while the monarch is in theory subject to the law,[9] in reality he is not under its control. While absolute power was granted the king in order to serve the law and its higher aims, monarchy does not have as part of its system controls to prevent abuse of power. The only assurance against corruption is the moral character of the king himself.[10] This is perhaps one reason that among the requirements of the king outlined in Deuteronomy is the writing of a Torah, as well as other specific limitations on power designed to encourage self-restraint. Given these safeguards, what is Abravanel's fear? It is that historical reality demonstrates the inherent risks of the monarchic form of government.[11]

Abravanel's claim of the superiority of government of the many is further supported by citing the principle of majority as accepted in matters of dispute in Talmudic law, as well as Aristotle's assertion that the truth is more readily arrived at by group process than by the efforts of one person.[12] He then proceeds to bring practical cases which buttress the theory he has outlined. Italian states such as Bologna, Genoa, Florence, and Venice, ruled by officials elected for a limited time, are better governed than the various monarchies, which are risky, dangerous, and can seriously harm a political community.[13]

Monarchy arises, according to Abravanel, not as the result of free election as in classical or contemporary republics, but as a consequence of violence and coercion. In the case of Israel, kingship was established at the request of an inexperienced people who believed the benefits would outweigh possible disadvantages. The request of the Israelites was founded upon the axiom that actions of the king would derive from his subordination to and adherence to the law. That is why, according to Abravanel, the Israelites asked Samuel, the judge-prophet, to select a king for them.

In general history, then, as in Jewish history, a contract or covenant between monarch and the people was made. The people expected the king to act in accordance with the law, while the king assumed his position of absolute power having pledged to use it to the advantage of the people. But there was a fatal flaw in this pact. Kings had almost routinely acted in bad faith, promising to maintain community interests as the highest priority, but falling captive to the weaknesses of ego aggrandizement, luxury, jealousy, and corruption. Abravanel is thus opposed to monarchy in its absolute or even limited manifestations, and argues against the philosophical legitimations which appear to support it.

To understand Abravanel's perspective, one must go back to the sources—classical, philosophical, and biblical—which influenced him. Primary among those whose thought led Abravanel in this anti-monarchist direction was Maimonides. Certainly no post-Maimonidean thinker could form a philosophical system or structure a political philosophy without advocating, modifying, or opposing that of Maimonides. As Leo Strauss has clearly demonstrated, Abravanel is "a strict, even passionate adherent of the literal interpretation of the *Guide of the Perplexed*."[14]

What does this mean? Maimonides and his Islamic contemporaries saw their task as the reconciliation of reason and revelation, a task facilitated by the fact that revelation, as understood by both traditions, was given in the form of law. Religious law, therefore, was seen to obligate one to pursue philosophy, to arrive at a characterization of the ideal political order. This order assumed, based on Plato's Republic, that the prophetic lawgiver was also a philosopher-king. The structure of Platonic political philosophy. permitted Maimonides to interpret revelation as putting forth a conception of the ideal political order the aim of which was to make possible, for those so endowed, the pursuit of philosophical truth. It is Leo Strauss' claim that the primary influence on Maimonides' view concerning the relation between revelation and philosophy derives from Plato's Laws.[15] While Judaism and Aristotelianism provide the content of Maimonides' teachings, Plato's philosophy furnishes the framework in which this content is developed.

Maimonides' attempt to reconcile Judaism with philosophy is based on the underlying identity—in his view—of the basic beliefs of the Jewish tradition with the essential concepts of philosophy. These latter are defined in the notion of ideal law, *i.e.,* law founded on philosophical truth. Maimonides wishes to demonstrate that Judaism consists of such laws.[16] But what of the laws in Judaism which are unphilosophical? How can they be understood? According to

Maimonides the assumption is that the text of the Hebrew Bible operates on two levels: the literal and the esoteric.

The literal meaning is addressed to the untutored, while the secret meaning is for those versed in philosophy. Both are necessary. The text as understood by the majority serves as a political tool for maintaining the happiness, stability, and sanctity of the Jewish community; this is Judaism with its traditional beliefs and rituals. The understanding and knowledge of philosophical truth, however, is reserved for those properly trained and able to discern it. Maimonides' reconciliation of Judaism and philosophy thus places on parallel tracks his deep religious belief and his extraordinary philosophical mind; that which connects them is the Pentateuch itself, and the Platonically structured political order which, according to Maimonides, the Torah espouses. The prophet, then, meets high intellectual standards; he is the philosopher-king *par excellence*.[17]

Abravanel strongly defends the literal understanding of the *Guide* and critiques Maimonides for what he sees as dangerous philosophical doctrines. He defends the legitimacy of Jewish tradition in the face of the more ambitious and even skeptical philosophical claims made, in the name of tradition, by Maimonides. Maimonides identified Judaism with perfect law in the Platonic sense, the prophet-lawgiver being the philosopher-king. But Abravanel decisively denies that philosophy is a constitutive element in prophecy. This means that the domain of the prophetic is much less a subject of political philosophy, which is thereby more restricted and limited.

In medieval Jewish thought, political philosophy could only be part of an understanding of Jewish law. Maimonides interpreted the Torah as a political tract concerned primarily with government and the establishment of a paradigmatic political order. Abravanel's literal reading of the *Guide* expresses a strong anti-rationalist tendency and leads to a devaluation of philosophy in general and political philosophy in particular. While for Maimonides the prophet, king and Messiah were the essential elements of political philosophy, Abravanel's anti-philosophical tendencies take him in another direction. For Maimonides, as indicated, the prophet is a philosopher-king, and the king subordinate to the highest court and the law it enforces; the Messiah is a political leader whose personal qualities, as both prophet and king, make him the Platonic philosopher-king *par excellence*. It is he who brings to realization on earth the possibility of a life devoted to the pursuit of knowledge.

Abravanel, however, claims the prophet not as philosopher but as "essentially supernatural."[18] And the Messiah is not a philosopher-king whose political and military skills diminish scarcity and conflict, thus allowing for increased pursuit of both human and Divine knowledge. Rather, having access, in some sense, to the Divine, he acts upon the world through miracles. It may indeed be stated that the anti-rationalism which informs Abravanel's opposition to monarchy is founded in a firm belief in miracles and miraculous providence.[19] Maimonides, although working within the parameters of Platonic philosophy, had accepted the Aristotelian premise that fundamentally the human being is a political creature; human beings naturally possess a political aspect, seeking to form both small and large communities and strike a balance between individual needs and social patterns. Abravanel, however, saw government as a concession to human weakness, originating in the sinful rebellion against Divine kingship. The "natural" state of the human being is to be compared with the Israelites' wanderings in the desert, where complete dependence on the miracles of Divine providence was requisite for survival.[20]

Maimonides, in contrast, construes this stage in Israelite history as transitional between slavery and political autonomy. For Abravanel, in contrast, the desert wandering was not a means to an end, but constituted a desirable end in itself.[21] Similarly, while Maimonides' Messiah establishes a stable society in which knowledge is pursued and love of the Divine thereby increased, Abravanel's Messiah restores the natural state of dependence, when human will and creativity are completely subordinated to Divine guidance. Maimonides' Messiah maintains the continuation of human history within parameters of justice, harmony and peace, while Abravanel's manifests an apocalyptic utopianism. The nature of Abravanel's Messiah is an outgrowth of his anti-monarchist propensity. The latter, in turn, derives in part from Abravanel's literalist, anti-rationalist reading of Maimonides *Guide for the Perplexed*.

Other forces also led Abravanel to take the decisive position that monarchy was not a preferred form of government. Some aver that the republicanism advocated by the early humanists influenced Abravanel. This is the position, for instance, of Yitzchak Baer.[22] Certainly Abravanel was familiar with humanist writings even before the years spent in Naples after the 1497 expulsion of the Jews from Portugal. Naples was a center of Italian humanism. Perhaps the Neo-Platonic movement in ferment in Italy at this time strengthened his anti-Aristotelianism. However, "the extent to which Abravanel was influenced—if influenced at all—by any of the Neapolitan spiritual leaders, is perhaps impossible to determine."[23]

One must also question the assumption that humanism as an intellectual movement consistently took an anti-monarchist position. While humanists, in their harking back to classical antiquity, greatly admired the Greek city-state and helped create semi-republics in Italy, the temporal monarchies of Europe were not uniformly disparaged. The aim of humanism was to defend human freedom, specifically intellectual freedom, against the dogmatism of the Church. Humanism *per se* did not fight against any specific political system in Europe, although it clearly opposed the narrowness and rigidity of the Church on philosophical and scientific questions. The fundamental institutions of medieval Europe—Church, feudalism, and empire—were seen as obstacles in the recovery of the classical spirit of humankind. But the humanists were generally conservative, unwilling to overthrow the temporal order and leave a political vacuum. They preferred gradual change through the influence of new ideas in the broader culture. Erasmus, for example, refused to support Luther;[24] Gianozzo Manetti extolled the civil function of religion; Pica della Mirandola advocated religious tolerance. The humanists were ardent admirers of classical antiquity and mighty opponents of medieval scholasticism and the Church's hold on the development of science; one cannot characterize them, however, as avid anti-monarchists. Humanism may have encouraged Abravanel to question the absolute power often held by a reigning monarch, but it would not constitute a primary factor in accounting for his strong anti-monarchism. Leo Strauss defines humanism as "going back from the tradition to the sources of the tradition.[25] But Abravanel's sources, Strauss avers, are "not so much the historians, poets, and orators of classical antiquity, but the literal sense of the Bible—and Josephus."[26]

Is Strauss correct? Does not Abravanel in his writings frequently refer to Plato and Aristotle, Seneca and Cicero? How might their views of government have influenced Abravanel? Plato's republic is much more a monarchy than a republic, a state in which the philosopher-king rules and the populace plays a negligible role in political processes.[27] Aristotle's *Politics* clearly asserts the legitimacy of monarchy as one of the many forms of government.[28] Seneca, adherent of Stoicism, and both tutor and advisor to the emperor Nero, viewed all human government as monarchical.[29] The king stood atop the hierarchy of which governments were naturally constituted, both representing and administering divine power. The practical virtue which Seneca sought was best attained for both individual and society within the political structure of monarchism.

It is Netanyahu's claim that some of Abravanel's language is strikingly similar to that found in Cicero's *Laws*.[30] Cicero's praise of monarchy is found most overtly in his *Republic,* which was not available to Abravanel in the fifteenth century,[31] but is also expressed, albeit in more subdued form in the *Laws*.[32] But Cicero also inveighed against tyrants, and Abravanel seems to have incorporated this critique as part of his anti-monarchist stance. However, Cicero's negative proclamations about tyranny are too weak a factor to account for the staunchness of Abravanel's attitude. Abravanel knew and was influenced by the historians and poets of antiquity and in his *Commentary* primarily argues against the classical concepts of monarchy rather than absorbing them as essential notions.

It seems unlikely, given the historical evidence, that Abravanel's personal experiences with monarchs led to his anti-monarchism. One could very well think it might have. Forced to flee Portugal in 1483 when a death sentence was issued against him by Joao II, expelled with his brethren from Spain in 1492, though a close advisor to Ferdinand I, Abravanel's most satisfactory relationship with a monarch seems to have been with Ferrante and Alfonso II of Naples.[33] Yet one does not find in the Commentary specific criticisms against Joao II and Ferdinand. Abravanel was cognizant of the unusual turns practical circumstances could take, and in general was personally well-treated by the monarchs he served.

Abravanel's anti-monarchism thus seems an anomaly. Earlier commentators on Deuteronomy and Samuel assumed a favorable attitude toward kingship in Israel, and they often went to great lengths to reconcile Samuel's sense of betrayal with the apparent commandment in Deuteronomy to institute monarchy.[34]

Abravanel's response to his predecessors points to an obvious discrepancy: if there was indeed a commandment to appoint a king, why didn't Joshua and the elders do so immediately upon taking possession of the land? Perhaps the Torah sought to distinguish between a constitutional monarch and an absolute despot, the former being required to write a sefer Torah, the latter abusing his power in the ways described by Samuel.[35] Yet Abravanel insists the sin in I Samuel was not a request for the wrong type of ruler, but the petition for any monarch other than God.[36] In addition, having rejected the rule of Samuel's sons, described as corrupt and despotic,[37] would the people's entreaties for a king have been motivated by the desire for an absolute ruler? Surely that seems unlikely. And if their desire was for a despot, would they not have bypassed Samuel's authority?[38] Abravanel, despite the traditions of his exegetical predecessors, understands I Samuel 8:6f as literally true and attempts to reconcile Deuteronomy 17:14f with it. Earlier commentators, however, accepted Deuteronomy 17:14f as a *mitzvah*, subsequently elaborating on I Samuel 8:6f in a manner consonant with that understanding.[39]

The source of Abravanel's unusual position must be seen, then, to lie elsewhere. Neither humanism, classical authorities, life experiences, nor traditional Jewish biblical commentators are sufficient to explain his uncommon view of monarchy. Abravanel likens the command to establish a king to that of *jafath toar*. Deuteronomy 21:10-14 describes the case of a soldier who sees among the captives a woman to whom he is attracted *jafath toar*. He is not required to take as wife an enemy woman captured in war; only if he desires her might he, under clearly delineated conditions, bring her to his home. Similarly, argues Abravanel, if the Jewish people desire a king, specific restrictions and safeguards apply. In neither case is the actual act preferred. Both the decision to live with a woman taken captive and that to institute monarchy are concessions to human weakness, permission to act upon one's desires if they cannot otherwise be controlled or satisfied. In both instances regulation is required; the very source of the actions is passion, necessitating rules to protect individual well-being and societal stability.

The commentators on Abravanel considered here, Leo Strauss and Benzion Netanyahu, concur that the probable source of Abravanel's anti-monarchist propensities lies in early medieval Christian thought.[40] Abravanel's notion of the government of the Jewish nation is that it consists of two parallel governments, "a government human and a government spiritual or divine."[41] This is "simply the Christian distinction between the authority spiritual and the authority temporal."[42] The head of the human government is not a monarch of the kind Abravanel criticized, but a charismatic leader, like Moses and the various judges. The authority temporal consists of a Lower Court, comprised of local judges, a Higher Court, or the Sanhedrin, and a leader, such as Moses. This tripartite temporal authority is paralleled by a similar hierarchy in the spiritual authority: the Levites, Priests and Prophets.[43] The ideal state is one in which a prophet-monarch reigns, not a philosopher-king. The monarchism against which Abravanel wrote was a temporal order, wrested from God as if by duress. It was not instituted, but conceded by God, and therefore is of diminished value. Made necessary by the development of cities, which Abravanel regarded as unnatural and the result of sin, the earthly monarch was both a symbol and a result of the propensity to sin. Pragmatist though he was in action, Abravanel's theoretical concept of monarchy harked back to an idealization of early Israelite life, when, in Buberian fashion, immediacy and dialogue characterized the individual-Divine encounter. Thus political life in the sense in which Abravanel knew it, *i.e.*, the life of the cities, most often governed by a king, was a compromise. As Netunyahu points out, Abravanel's division of realms into spiritual and temporal precisely parallels Augustine's *City of God and City of Man*, in which the aim of human existence is to increase the power and scope of the City of God, until God's dominion triumphs. While for Abravanel the establishment of a monarchy might be beneficial for other nations, for Israel it constituted an overt rejection of the Divine Kingdom. Abravanel's ideal state is a theocracy in which homage is given to God, not to a human ruler. Law formulated by human beings usually led to tyranny and injustice; therefore Divine law must prevail. Abravanel did not view human autonomy as consonant with freewill and God's challenge to human capacities as did Maimonides. He preferred, instead, the model of a completely dependent relationship. In this sense Abravanel moves back to an early, if not pre-medieval, understanding of the tradition. His desire was to know precisely that which revelation taught.

By preferring in this spirit the sources of the tradition to the tradition itself, he can scarcely avoid the danger of coming into conflict with the teaching of tradition.[44]

Abravanel's political theory stands apart from that of other medieval Jewish thinkers. The consummate statesman, diplomat, and financier, Abravanel was a man of history. The historical perspective he brought to his *Commentary* added a new dimension to the methodology of biblical exegesis. Yet somehow Abravanel could not envisage that Torah would support, indeed encourage, a form of government in which tyranny, corruption, and injustice were not only possible, but also almost inescapable. Thus his model was not the realm of active human struggle, but a more passive framework, that of immediate dependence upon Divine guidance. It has been said that Abravanel "was . . . the first Jew who became deeply influenced by Christian political thought."[45]

One might also conjecture that the fate of his people during the turbulent and terrible years at the close of the fifteenth century led Abravanel to rely more on God's immediate intervention than upon the seemingly invisible rise toward human progress, political stability, and ultimate justice for the Jewish people.

NOTES

1. Jews were expelled from England in 1290, while the French expulsion took place in 1306. In Germany, Jews surviving the Crusades were never officially expelled due to the lack of a central authority. "The larger significance of the Spanish Expulsion lay in the fact that, as a result, Western Europe had been emptied of Jews." Yosef H. Yerushalmi, *Zachor: Jewish History and Jewish Memory* (New York: Schocken, 1989), 59-60.

2. Estimates vary. A generally accepted figure is around 200,000. See Jacob R. Marcus, *The Jew in the Medieval World* (New York: Atheneum, 1938), 52.

3. See, for example, Benzion Netanyahu, *Don Isaac Abravanel: Statesman and Philosopher* (Philadelphia: Jewish Publication Society, 1972), 162, 176, 187, 190; Leo Strauss, "On Abravanel's Philosophical Tendency and Political Teaching," in *Isaac Abravanel: Six Lectures,* ed. J.B. Trend and H.M.J. Loewe (Cambridge University Press, 1937), 95, 107, 110. ". . . he is a humanist who uses his classical learning to confirm his thoroughly medieval conceptions rather than to free himself from them." Strauss, 128.

4. Netanyahu, 190-260.

5. See Gerald J. Blidstein, "The Monarchic Imperative in Rabbinic Perspective," *Association of Jewish Studies Review* 7-8 (1982-83): 15-39. Cf. Nahmanides, *Commentary on the Torah,* ed. C.B. Chavel 2 Jerusalem: Mosad Harav Kook, 1960): 424 (Hebrew).

6. Nahmanides, *Commentary on the Torah* 2:424 (Hebrew). He follows the view of R. Judah in T.B. Sanhedrin 20b, not that of R. Nehorai.

7. He means Aristotle and his medieval disciples. See Abravanel, I Samuel, 8:6 in *Commentary on the Prophets* 1 (Jerusalem: Torah Vadaath, 1956): 203 (Hebrew). It is Strauss' view (112, n. 4) that Abravanel was familiar with these texts from Christian, Jewish, and Islamic sources.

8. Cf. Abravanel's view of the rights of the people under a tyrant king in *Commentary on Deuteronomy* 17:16-20. When accepting a king, the people have made a covenant with him, promising their obedience. That covenant is regarded as absolute.

9. Netanyahu quotes Nicolas of Cusa: "The prince must rule according to the law, and is supreme only with respect to matters which are not clearly defined by the law." Netanyahu, 176.

10. Aristotle, Cicero and Seneca, all of whose political writings influenced medieval political conceptions, insisted that moral excellence is a *sine qua non* of authentic kingship.

11. See *Commentary,* I Samuel, 8:4.

12. While Aristotle asserted this, however, he also advocated monarchy. See *Politics*, Book 3, chap. 9-11 which Abravanel quotes in his *Commentary* on I Samuel, 8:4.

13. Netanyahu, 204-205.

14. Strauss, 101.

15. Ibid., 96-99.

16. See Maimonides, *The Guide of the Perplexed*, trans. Shlomo Pines, 2 (Chicago: University of Chicago Press, 1969): Chapters 32-48, 360-412.

17. Loc cit.

18. Strauss, 107, 110 n. 4.

19. Maimonides strongly influenced Spinoza's political philosophy as put forth in the *Theologico-Political Treatise*. See Leo Strauss, *Spinoza's Critique of Religion*, trans. E.M. Sinclair. (New York: Schocken, 1965); also L. Roth, *Spinoza, Descartes, and Maimonides* (Oxford: Clarendon Press, 1924); H.A. Wolfson, *The Philosophy of Spinoza* (New York: Meridian Books, 1960, 1934).

20. Spinoza, of course, began the *Theologio-Political Treatise* with a critique of prophecy (chapter one) and of miracles (chapter six). He attempted to unhinge the connection of philosophy and religion made by Maimonides. Spinoza denigrated religion in the name of philosophy and the pursuit of reason. Abravanel, however, moved in the other direction, understanding history to be determined almost entirely by Divine providence. Philosophy, reason, and human will could be but minimal factors.

21. Cf. Martin Buber, *The Kingship of God*, trans. Richard Scheimann (New York: Harper Torchbooks, ·1973), esp. chapter two; also Rochelle Landesman Millen, *Martin Buber as Interpreter of the Bible* (Unpublished dissertation, McMaster University, 1984), chapter 4, esp. 252-53.

22. Yitchak Baer, *History of The Jews in Christian Spain* 1 (Philadelphia: Jewish Publication Society, 1966): 256-57.

23. Netanyahu, 66.

24. He did not, however, systematically oppose monarchy. While some of his writings expose the corruption of absolute power, and rulers like Alexander the Great and Julius Caesar are attacked for the wars and tragedies they brought upon many, Erasmus did not advocate insurrection against the king. Rather, his *Education of a Christian Prince* suggested that proper training could diminish the dangers of absolutism.

25. Strauss, 127.

26. Loc. cit.

27. Netanyahu maintains that it is unlikely Plato's statements in the *Laws* in favor of a government integrating monarchic and democratic elements influenced Abravanel. See Netanyahu, 308, n. 66.

28. "The true forms of government, therefore, are those in which the one, or the few, or the many govern with a view to the common interest. . . . Of forms of government in which one rules, we call that . . . kingship or royalty . . ." Aristotle, *Politics*, in *The Basic Works of Aristotle*, trans. Richard

McKeon 3 (New York: Random House, 1971): 7, (1279a 28-35). Regarding Abravanel's knowledge of the *Politics* see Strauss, 105, n. 3. Cf. n. 12 above.

29. Samuel Dill, *Roman Society: From Nero to Marcus Aurelius* (New York: Macmillan, 1956), 289-333.

30. Netanyahu, 185.

31. Loc. cit.

32. *Laws*, Book 3, Chapter 2, quoted by Netanyahu.

33. He also enjoyed a long period of stability and prosperity as advisor to Alfonso V of Portugal, who died in 1481. With Joao II's accession to the throne, the situation for Jews in Portugal became precarious.

34. See Sifre on Deuteronomy 17:14, Tosefta Sanhedrin 20b, Nahmanides on Genesis 49:10. Some of their comments are: Samuel's anger was against the description of Israelite kingship as "like all the nations" rather than opposition to monarchy as such; or the people's request manifested scorn for God's appointed, the prophet and judge Samuel.

35. I Samuel, 8:11-18.

36. Abravanel, *Commentary*.

37. I Samuel, 8:5.

38. Abravanel, *Commentary*.

39. An exception is Ibn Ezra, who says the passage expresses permission, not the obligation of *mitzvah*.

40. See Strauss, 122-129, and Netanyahu, 159, 189-194.

41. Strauss, 124.

42. Loc. cit.

43. Netanyahu writes, "The similarity between this conception and the major political theory of medieval Christendom suggests itself very strongly," but it is "conspicuously anachronistic, for at the time when Abravanel wrote his commentaries the concept of the 'temporal' and 'spiritual,' powers had become almost outdated." Netanyahu, 159.

44. Strauss, 128.

45. Ibid., 126.

Judaizing Women in Castile:
A Look at Their Lives Before and After 1492

Renée Levine Melammed

The year 1391 was a watershed in the history of the Jews of Spain. Tens of thousands of Jews were subjected to forced conversion, resulting in the creation of a large group of converted Jews or *conversos*.[1] While all had been baptized, the majority of them were far from enthusiastic about the new religion that had been acquired under duress. This mass conversion was not the result of any systematic indoctrination or of an orderly, pre-planned process. On the contrary, it had been carried out haphazardly and had spread indiscriminately; the final results were devastating for all involved.

Thus families as well as communities were in disarray; because there had been no grand plan, no one—not the Spanish Church, the Jewish rabbis, the monarchy, or the masses—knew how to proceed.[2] While some of the converts accepted their new reality and the supremacy of the Church, there were, nonetheless, those converts who attempted to disregard the fait accompli, and chose to continue observing Judaism. Some ninety years later, the latter group would be categorized by the Inquisition as judaizers or *judaizantes,* were accused of heresy and forced to stand trial.

Information regarding judaizing between 1391, the time of these forced baptisms, and 1478, the date of the establishment of the Spanish Inquisition, is somewhat limited. While judaizing obviously demeaned the sanctity of the sacrament of baptism, no legal actions against those doing so were taken by the Church prior to 1478. While efforts most certainly were made not to flaunt one's proclivities publicly, we do know that there were numerous ties between conversos and members of the remaining Jewish community.[3] Some examples of such contact are the making of donations of oil for the lamps in the synagogue; purchasing kosher meat at Jewish butcheries; and obtaining *masah* on Passover from members of the Jewish community; these and others will be discussed presently. However, vis-à-vis documentation concerning the Jewishness of the conversos for the period between 1391 and 1478, the historian is faced with rather limited alternatives. One option is to consult rabbinic responsa, the recorded questions and answers which reflect specific legal or halakhic problems encountered by individuals in the Jewish community. This material deals mainly with communities outside of the Iberian Peninsula, and highlights problems that arose due to the presence of converso exiles re-entering Jewish communities. Unfortunately, the responsa are neither comprehensive enough nor sufficiently reliable for assessing actual judaizing of those first generations of conversos who were still living on Spanish soil.[4]

On the other hand, the nature of the material available changes drastically once the Inquisition was established. If seeking judaizing conversos, or in this case, conversas, one encounters myriads of documents pertaining to trials aiming to uncover this very same crypto-Judaism. However, before looking at this phenomenon as reflected in Inquisition documents, whether prior or subsequent to the Expulsion of the Jewish community in 1492, the phenomenon of crypto-Judaism itself must be considered.

This very term, crypto-Judaism, denotes the existence of a clandestine religion which could not be identical to Judaism, and thus its practices are characterized by lacunae as well as by addenda. At the same time, the ever present threat of the Inquisition must not be overlooked; never knowing who was a potential informer made observance difficult and dangerous, even in one's own home. Consequently, the crypto-Jew faced a double challenge: how to successfully observe and how to simultaneously ensure the utmost secrecy. In addition, the reality was that pre-1492, judaizers were able to turn to the Jewish community for support, whether moral, religious, educational, or economic.

This relationship stands in sharp contrast to the post-1492 situation. The Inquisition was established in 1478 and the Jews were expelled fourteen years later.[5] After 1492, no longer was there a living example of Judaism or a source of support; crypto-Judaism had been stripped of all the accoutrements of normative Judaism. No longer were there religious leaders, educators, ritual functionaries or literature. In addition, the time factor and the fact that this religious knowledge would have to be transmitted orally must be taken into account; the crypto-Jew would have only his or her fallible memory upon which to rely.

One needs to weigh the options available to these judaizers and to determine where a judaizer might observe, hopefully, without being noticed. The home, the only remaining institution, was the logical choice, although even within the confines of one's own abode, by no means was safety guaranteed. One must consider the fact that the average home had numerous servants whose turnover rate as employees was considerable. As a result, a pool of potential informants existed, many of whom could describe in detail the daily activities of their present or former employers.[6] Yet despite the various internal and external dangers, many judaizers continued to observe. In the crypto-Jewish society under discussion, the women, traditionally responsible for maintaining the home, assume a more active role than previously held in Jewish society; they are especially concerned with transmitting the Jewish heritage and stand out in this society in their role as teachers.[7]

When comparing pre- and post-1492 judaizing, two related difficulties arise: one of periodization and one of relegating observances to specific periods. Concerning periodization, one would assume that the date for a logical dividing line would be 1492 and in fact, vis-à-vis trials held between 1478 and 1491, no problem arises in utilizing such a construct. While the defendants in these trials might include conversos who may have chosen Catholicism on their own, the majority were descendants of the forced converts of 1391; in other words, they were third, fourth, or fifth generation conversos who were being accused of judaizing. This pre-1492 period is not particularly problematic and, as will become evident, observance during this time was often characterized by ties to the pre-Expulsion Jewish community.

A problem arises, however, in the following period. Because a trial was held after 1492, it does not necessarily mean that the defendant's judaizing occurred after that date, for various other possibilities exist. For instance, information might have reached the Holy Tribunal years after the actual practice of "heretical" acts on the part of the baptized Jew or descendant of Jews occurred. The judaizer was still held responsible for these actions, although if he or she had desisted in the interim, the tribunal would probably have taken this into account. Again, although the trial transpired after 1492, its proceedings would reveal judaizing dating to the earlier period.

Likewise, one must take into consideration the role played by the stage in the inquisitorial process known as the Grace Period.[8] Prior to setting up an Inquisitorial Court, there was an "open house" policy which could last a few weeks or as long as a few months. During this time, notaries were available to record confessions as well as relevant information from anyone and everyone. This was a means of amassing data from informers and confessants alike, enabling the prosecution to organize its cases. Many conversos appeared and offered confessions; absolution was immediately granted, although the confessants were duly warned about the future: a relapsed heretic should expect no mercy.

The first courts of the Inquisition in Castile were set up in 1481 in Seville, in 1482 in Córdoba, and in 1483 in Ciudad Real. The third court, serving Ciudad Real and environs, Campo de Calatrava and the Archdiocese of Toledo, moved its headquarters to Toledo in 1485. During the Grace Periods, the fear of repercussions led many judaizing conversos in Castile to come forth and confess. Having done so, these confessants considered themselves to be out of danger. Nevertheless, it is amazing to see how often the Inquisition later returned to investigate the sincerity of some of these same conversos, in order to determine if they had indeed upheld their promise to be penitent. If there was the slightest doubt, that reconciled converso found him or herself to be a defendant on trial. Needless to say, these confessions, most of which were recorded in the 1480's, would be cited at the onset of the trial. Then information would be amassed to show that the defendant had relapsed, serving as proof of a second round of judaizing; this pattern can be discerned among some of these conversas. In short, this type of post-1492 trial provides information about judaizing prior to the Expulsion in the form of a confession, and might possibly contain references to later judaizing as well.

Predictably, the encounter with the post-1492 conversos is less ambiguous. Of the two groups that emerge during this period, the first comprises those who chose to convert in 1492 rather than to leave their homeland. Obviously, they would only have had contact with the Inquisition after 1492. This is, so-to-speak, the last "wave" of converts; essentially, all who converted at this time had had contact with Jews, for they had been bona fide Jews themselves.

The second group encompasses those conversos who were born after 1492 or who had been extremely young at the time of the Expulsion. These individuals experienced the greatest disadvantage, that of never having seen a practicing Jew and having no personal memory from which to draw, thus solely relying on the memories of those who taught them about their heritage. This group presents no complications in terms of periodization or of dating their observances: all of their judaizing experiences occurred after 1492.

Consequently, the various examples of judaizing women from Castile to be presented have been arranged into three groups: those who were tried before 1492; those whose activities overlap the so-called cut-off date of 1492; and those of the sixteenth century who can be unquestionably distanced from the pre-1492 converso experience.

Information about the members of the first group, whose judaizing preceded the Expulsion, includes detailed records from various early trials that, at times, closely resemble descriptions of normative Jewish homes. For example, María Díaz of Ciudad Real was tried from 1483-4.[9] The specifics of her judaizing activities included honoring the Sabbath by lighting candles, preparing food in advance, wearing clean clothes, not engaging in work, visiting relatives and friends, and praying and reading to others from a prayerbook. (Her sister, Leonor González had joined her at these sessions and during the riots and looting that occurred in Ciudad Real in 1474, Hebrew books were discovered in Leonor's house.)[10] María observed Jewish fasts including Yom Kippur, ate meat slaughtered Jewishly, and when not possible to obtain kosher meat, ate fruit and eggs. On Passover, she either bought new dishes or ritually soaked or boiled them, attended a *seder* and ate *masah*. This conversa observed the Festivals of *Cinquesma* or Shavuot, the holiday signifying the day when the law was given; the Festival of the Booths or Sukkot; the Festival of the Candles or Hanukah; and the Festival of the Horn, or Rosh Ha-shana, the New Year. María even had a Hebrew name. After fleeing Ciudad Real to Palma, near Córdova, for about seven months, Leonor instructed conversas there where, among other activities, she administered a ritual bath for the purification of a maiden on her wedding day.

This case is particularly interesting as there is no detailed confession but rather a most impressive and convincing witness for the prosecution. He too was a New Christian, in this case, none other than an ex-rabbi who had converted and, therefore, was extremely familiar with the activities engaged in by this conversa.[11]

Catalina López, also of Ciudad Real, was tried posthumously from 1484-5. The information presented in this trial reveals that she was practicing Judaism as early as 1434. This conversa had observed Yom Kippur, breaking her fast with a meat meal, and as late as the 1470's, was hosting prayer groups in her home on Yom Kippur; she had possession and made use of a prayerbook. Her Sabbath observance included bathing on Fridays, preparing food including special Sabbath stews, lighting candles, and wearing clean clothes. She had celebrated

Sukkot for nine days and had participated in Jewish mourning rituals: she washed the dead, sat in mourning for nine days on the floor, and ate fish and eggs at the traditional post-burial meal.[12]

María Alonso was a third neighbor who, although still alive at the time of her trial, had disappeared. She was, however, apprehended while her 1484-5 trial was in process. During the proceedings, witnesses claimed that the defendant's house had been a meeting place for conversas whom she instructed in Judaism. María observed the Sabbath by preparing food before its onset and eating it cold on Saturday; she also abstained from work, lit candles, wore clean clothes and paid visits to fellow conversos. She had been seen praying, often in the homes of one of the other converso leaders, and had been facing the wall while engaged in such prayer. María and her sister, Catalina de Zamora, bathed the dead and made them shrouds, and were also keeners of Jewish dirges.[13]

While Ciudad Real was a center of converso and conversa judaizing, similar activities transpired in neighboring villages and cities. For example, Beatriz González of Toledo confessed in 1487 that in her youth she had seen her mother pray on Yom Kippur and that she had been taught by her to fast. Sometimes the two women bathed and cut their nails in preparation for this solemn day; they alway donned clean clothes and went barefoot. In addition, they lit candles and asked forgiveness of each other and of their close friends and relatives. Beatriz related how she went to synagogue to "see how the candles burned and how the Jews prayed, for I heard them."[14] On the holiday of Passover, she baked *masah*, often distributing it to relatives and friends, but sometimes buying it or receiving it as a gift. She participated in a *seder*, in which lettuce and parsley were eaten with "sauce," most likely salt water.[15] She confessed that during the festival of Sukkot, she had occasionally entered the booths of Jews and ate fruit there; the prosecutor claimed that she had even built a *sukkah* or booth on her own property.[16]

The presence of a Jewish community was clearly an asset for the judaizing converso. In the trial of Elvira López of Talamanca, this conversa invited Jews to *hadas*, the Sephardi celebration traditionally held on the eighth night after the birth of a male or female child. This information was provided in 1491 by none other than one of the Jewish guests himself.[17]

Once the focus shifts to the trials that transpired after 1492, the second group under discussion, there are obviously no more of these rare Jewish witnesses; yet the shadow of the Jewish presence lingers. A different Elvira López, a resident of San Gil, confessed in 1492 that she and her husband rented houses to Jews and had received gifts from them including *masah*, which the couple then ate.[18] She also partook of the post-burial meal or *cohuerzo*, eating olives, eggs and fish. Elvira also mentioned an unusual indulgence: she would buy meat not only in Jewish shops, but from Moslem butcheries as well.[19]

In 1493, Blanca Rodríguez of Guadalajara was accused of fasting on Yom Kippur as did the Jews, and of remaining with them for the entire Day of Atonement.[20] In the same year, 1493, Blanca's neighbor, Mencía Rodríguez, was accused of sending contributions of oil to the synagogue in order to save her soul. In addition, she would go there to clean and adorn the synagogue's lamps, placing wicks in them and pouring oil inside.[21] Inés Rodríguez of Illescas was accused in 1498 of going to the Kol Nidre services on Yom Kippur eve, for she believed that her sins would be forgiven.[22] Juana Rodríguez of Toledo confessed in 1498 that she fasted on Yom Kippur in the hope of obtaining riches as well as a husband.[23] In addition, in honor of the Jewish law, she lent Jews a rug and a bordered sheet for their *sukkah*; she was hoping that this would procure her salvation.[24]

The trial of María González of Casarrubios del Monte, held in 1500, reveals that the defendant engaged in a great deal of judaizing as well as contact with the Jewish community. This conversa usually prepared meals for the Sabbath day, but when she did not do so, she sent her servant to a Jewish home in search of stew. María observed Yom Kippur, the holiday of Sukkot, the Jewish mourning period or *shiva*, and abstained from eating *trefa* or non-kosher foods. She baked *hallah* and sometimes baked *masah* for Passover; when she did not do so, her husband sent flour to a Jew whom he paid to prepare the unleavened bread for them. She had also sent a servant in search of *masah* as well as other foods needed for the first night of the holiday. María bought meat from the Jewish butchery, obtained kosher wine from Jews, lent clothing to them for their holidays, donated material for shrouds, and went to see a rabbi before she gave birth. After menstruating and post-partum, she bathed and placed clean sheets on her bed.[25] Here is a picture of the life of an observant crypto-Jewess extremely dependent upon the Jewish community for support and provisions. Although she was tried after 1492, the fact that there were such obvious ties to the Jewish community proves that her activities as well as those of many other judaizing conversas were clearly related to the pre-Expulsion period.

Thus Catalina Sánchez of Madrid, tried from 1502-3, was charged with asking Jews for *masah* at Passover time.[26] Beatriz Jarada of Chinchón was tried from 1506-7 and accused of not working on Yom Kippur, which she had observed in the hope of attaining salvation, and of observing Passover, when she ate *masah* which she brought from the Jews.[27] Elvira López of Toledo's confession of 1485 appears in her trial of 1510-11. She explained that she had observed Yom Kippur, being taught by her mother at the age of twelve, and had continued to do so even after marrying; later her husband joined her. She had eaten *masah* given to her by Jews in exchange for fruit, and had, in preparation for interment, bathed various deceased members of her family, including her father. Finally, she had lent some material to a Jew making a *sukkah* so that he could properly observe the festival.[28] As can be discerned, most and sometimes all of the information revealed in these post-1492 trials relates to judaizing activities before the Expulsion. In many of them, the only proof available was the confession provided by the defendant during a Grace Period which had occurred years earlier. As mentioned earlier, the conversa would have confessed in order to reconcile herself to the Church and to avoid facing a trial, but the Inquisition often suspected that the confessant had withheld information at the time of confession or had been insincere at the time of reconciliation and had then reverted to crypto-Judaism. In fact, these judaizers had often been trying to determine precisely how much or which information would satisfy the inquisitor, how many observances or which particular ones would suffice in order to appear to be a sinner who would be eligible for reconciliation. Thus it is not surprising to learn that some may have intentionally neglected to mention certain activities, and that others, among them repentant confessing conversas, had continued to judaize.

Many of the confessions cited above were recorded during the Grace Period in 1486, as were all of the instances which follow. Juana Gómez of Alcázar, who was tried in 1496, only mentioned Passover observance, at which time she partook of *masah* and used new vessels for food and drink.[29] Blanca Díaz of Ocaña, who was tried from 1511-3, said that her female in-laws told her to fast on Yom Kippur so that the Lord would fulfill her wishes as well as grant her forgiveness.[30] Elvira Núñez of Toledo, who was tried in 1501, bathed the day before Yom Kippur, asked for forgiveness from her family and went barefoot on this Day of Atonement.[31] María García of Herrera, tried from 1500-1, confessed to the identical Yom Kippur preparations and observances as did Elvira, and added that after menstruation and birth, she slept in a separate bed from her husband until she had bathed.[32] María López of La Membrilla, who was tried from 1512-22, confessed to the same acts of ritual purity, to fasting and asking forgiveness on Yom Kippur, to hearing prayers read from Jewish books, to eating *masah* as secretly as possible, and to partaking of post-burial meals of fish and eggs.[33] A final example from this group that confessed in 1486 is María Alfonso of Herrera who was tried from 1500-1. Her report was extremely detailed and included the act of cutting her nails and discarding them in the fire the night before Yom Kippur, at which time she went barefoot and fasted; she also engaged in other fasts. María wore clean clothes in honor of Passover, lit candles and baked and ate *masah*. She bathed the deceased in her family, and ate a meatless meal on the floor following burials.[34]

One must keep in mind the fact that these trials took place between four and twenty years after the Expulsion, in other words, between ten and twenty-six years after the original confessions had been made. In this light, it is all the more surprising to discover a trial held from 1530-1 in which the only convincing information about judaizing is the defendant's confession of 1485. Inés González of Toledo explained that her mother-in-law, Aldonza de Herrera, taught her to judaize in 1460; at the time of her statement, she had been a crypto-Jewess for twenty-five years. Among her activities were lighting Sabbath candles, preparing and eating Sabbath meals and wearing clean clothes on the Sabbath and holidays. She fasted on Yom Kippur, when she would ask forgiveness of others; she observed other fast days as well. Inés ate *masah* when the Jews ate it, and consumed meat slaughtered by Jewish ceremony. When a relative died, she observed the period of mourning, sitting at a low table, ate eggs and fish and, when appropriate, sent food to other mourners. She had blessed her children and grandchildren in the Jewish manner, and they then kissed her hand. Lastly, Inés confessed to having donated to charity, in particular, having given money to the Jews for oil and lending them her jewels to wear during the holidays.[35]

On the other hand, the trial of Teresa de Acre exemplifies a case in which an additional confession revealed information not provided in the first testimony. In 1485, Teresa had only mentioned observing mourning rituals such as eating at *cohuerzo* meals held in relatives' homes. However, when tried from 1493-4, she confessed again. Teresa returned to the topic of mourning, during which time she had eaten at low tables after the funerals of her in-laws; then she revealed that she had gone to sit in the *sukkah* of Jewish neighbors, eating fruit with them.[36] Obviously, additions of this nature only convinced the Inquisitors that conversos were indeed withholding information at the time of these voluntary confessions.

Lest one assumes that all of the trials that transpired during the first score or two following the Expulsion dealt only with pre-1492 judaizing, a few examples should serve to dispel any misconceptions. Isabel Alvarez of Toledo had been reconciled in the 1480's; at her trial in 1497, she admitted that she had returned to her former sinful ways and had fasted on Yom Kippur the previous year as well as on other occasions.[37] In 1486, Mayor González of Herrera confessed, among other things, to fasting, observing Yom Kippur while barefoot, having bathed the day before and refraining from work on that day; she had separated herself from her husband after menstruating until she had bathed. In 1500, she confessed that again she had been told to fast, and did so after donning a clean blouse; in addition, she began to observe the Sabbath and dietary laws again.[38] Juana Ruíz of Daimiel, who had been reconciled to the Church pre-1492, was accused in 1503 of once again observing the Sabbath and of fasting on Yom Kippur after her reconciliation.[39] Fasts are central to the trial of Juana Gómez of Alcázar in 1513. She had confessed in 1486 to asking for forgiveness on Yom Kippur, listening to her father read from a prayerbook, and eating (or not eating) as he did on that day.[40] Twenty-seven years later, she was accused of continuing to fast on Yom Kippur as well as on other traditional fast days.[41]

The next case appears in a fascinating file which dates from 1530 and contains the confessions of five of the six members of a judaizing family from Toledo.[42] The father, Gómez García de Torrijos, was none other than a vassal of the commander of a military order. In 1485, he confessed to observing Yom Kippur, removing fat from meat, wearing a clean shirt on the Sabbath and to allowing his wife and daughters to observe Jewish laws.[43] His wife Aldonza Gómez confessed to the same observances as did her spouse, adding that she let her daughters fast on Yom Kippur.[44] One daughter, Elvira, of marriageable age in 1485 and deceased by the time of the trial in 1530, claimed that her mother ordered her to light candles on the Sabbath, to fast on Yom Kippur and to remove the fat from meat.[45] A younger daughter, Catalina, also cited her mother as having told her to light candles and to observe the Sabbath and Yom Kippur, to remove fat from meat and to pray from a psalter.[46] The defendant and oldest daughter, Mayor, was thirty years of age at the time of these confessions and reconciliations. She admitted that she had fasted on

Yom Kippur and had seen her mother and sisters observe the Sabbath, especially by lighting candles. Mayor testified that she had begun judaizing at the age of fourteen and had practiced these Jewish rites for about eight years, but desisted when she contracted her first marriage in 1479.[47]

The Inquisition chose to recall Mayor in 1530, who by this time, was a seventy-five year old woman. She was accused of having given false testimony, and of observing Jewish law not only when she was single, but as a married woman as well. The prosecutor claimed, among other charges, that she had worn clean blouses on the Sabbath, lit candles, removed fat from meat, eaten *masah* on Passover, and attended *cohuerzos* while seated at a low table. He emphasized that her Yom Kippur as well as mourning observances took place while she was married.[48] Although old and frail according to her daughter's testimony and plea of 1530, Mayor was subjected to torture, at which time she revealed nothing.[49] The Tribunal decided that the prosecutor had not proven his contentions; consequently, while her punishment would entail public humiliation and chastisement, Mayor was to be treated as a penitent.[50]

Accounts of relapsing and judaizing anew rarely appear in trials at such a late date; actually, if the Inquisition had even considered re-investigating these self-confessed judaizers of the fifteenth century, most were no longer alive to face interrogation. Rather than to prosecute posthumous offenders in the sixteenth century, the Tribunal found itself quite busy with first-time offenders as early as 1500. At this time, there was a young maiden-prophetess named Inés of Herrera who was particularly convincing in her ways. She managed to catalyze a small messianic movement as did another young girl, María of Chillón; a few additional charismatic conversos had similar experiences. Once the Inquisition heard about these developments, it mobilized its forces to quickly and effectively extirpate this local heretical menace.[51] Unsurprisingly, conversos have historically been particularly susceptible to messianic tidings; between 1499 and 1502, many were brought to trial on charges such as having fasted on Mondays and Thursdays in the hopes of being redeemed and of going to the Promised Land.[52] However, since this phenomenon is well-known, the cases of some lesser known judaizing women of sixteenth-century Castile will be presented.

In 1513, Leonor Núñez y Núñez of Alcázar confessed to fasting and asking forgiveness of others on Yom Kippur. She was accused of joining other judaizers in order to observe this September fast and of going barefoot.[53] Fasting was also the only observance confessed to by Catalina Gómez of Toledo in 1515; she would appear for meals, but refrain from eating.[54] In 1516, a mother and daughter from Cogolludo were accused concomitantly. Both were charged with eating or preparing Sabbath stews, removing the fat from meat prior to kashering it, and refraining from eating non-kosher meat and fish. The daughter, Isabel López, was also charged with dressing up and praying on the Sabbath.[55] Numerous servants who had worked for María López and her daughter testified regarding their judaizing.[56]

During this very same period (1516-1518), a clergyman attested to the unconventional practices of María Alvarez of Buitrago; he had inadvertently seen her in mourning some three or four years before, although at the time, he was not aware of the significance of her actions.[57] In 1518, Elvira Díaz of Toledo was accused of joining her family in order to observe Yom Kippur, at which time they asked forgiveness of one another.[58] The 1520-3 trial of Isabel García of Hita is rich with information: she observed the Sabbath, wearing clean and festive clothes, preparing food beforehand and eating it cold in the company of others. In addition, she placed new wicks, more than usual, in her lamps, and lit them earlier on Friday nights. Isabel kashered meat, and mourned as would a Jew. She washed the bodies of the deceased in the Jewish manner, visited other mourners, and when her husband died in 1513, she was said to have confined herself to her room for an entire year. The description of her keening and mourning is clearly based on her perception of Jewish law and include her own embellishments.[59]

Another conversa from Hita was tried from 1520-1. Beatriz López was accused of observing the Sabbath, dressing in clean and festive clothes, and lighting lamps early on Friday nights when she would also retire earlier than usual. She was condemned for having partaken of *adafina* stews and other Jewish food, kashering her meat and for strictly adhering to the dietary laws.[60] According to the prosecution, Mayor Meléndez of Guadalajara seemed to be mainly concerned with lighting Sabbath candles and with avoiding consumption of pork, meat with blood, and bacon; she would leave the room if there was bacon or lard cooking.[61] In 1538, Leonor Gutiérrez of Hita was apparently bringing more oil to her house on Fridays than was customary to bring on other days. In addition, she ordered the servants to retire before she and her husband did; the intention was to avoid detection of the fact that the lamp was not being extinguished.[62]

Lastly, some examples of conversas tried for judaizing can be found in two trials held almost a century after the Expulsion. In the course of these trials, which both began in 1590, numerous conversos, most of them residents of Alcázar, testified.[63] In order to illustrate the judaizing that transpired in this crypto-Jewish community in the second half of the sixteenth century, the confessions of four conversas will be cited. The first, Isabel de la Vega, had been instructed in Judaism by various women, including her own mother. In honor of the Sabbath, she changed bed linens on Friday; cleaned the oil lamp, placing clean wicks in it after discarding the oil; allowed the wicks to burn down to the end; dressed up, wearing a clean blouse; prepared food in advance; and refrained from work. In honor of Passover, she would bathe and eat *masah*. In accordance with the purity laws, she bathed after menstruating and discarded nail clippings and fallen hairs into a burning fire. Lastly, Isabel referred to observing the New Month, or Rosh Hodesh.[64]

María de la Vega, probably a cousin of Isabel's, also provided a surprisingly rich description of crypto-Jewish life in Alcázar. The confessant's mother as well as another conversa had initiated María into Judaism at the age of ten. Consequently, she observed the Sabbath by changing the bed linens, cleaning and changing the wicks in the lamp, and by praying. María ate no pork, washed meat thoroughly, rinsing off all blood, and ate poultry that was beheaded ceremonially. She fasted on Thursdays and on Yom Kippur and ate *masah* on Passover.[65]

Similar observances are found in the confession of Catalina López who rested on the Sabbath, washed meat carefully, and observed the New Month and three annual festivals as well. The first holiday, she noted, fell close to the date of the holiday of Easter; the second was in May and the third in September. Presumably these were the three pilgrimage festivals of Passover, Shavuot and Sukkot.[66] Lastly, Beatriz Ruíz related in 1590 that her mother taught her to observe the Sabbath, to light candles, not to eat pork and to celebrate some of the festivals.[67]

In conclusion, there is no doubt that the presence of the Jewish community was extremely influential in the development of the Spanish crypto-Jewish community. A look at the lives of judaizers before 1492 as well as the study of trials held after the Expulsion attest to the strong ties that existed between the two groups and to the dependence of converso judaizers upon their Jewish brethren for reinforcement, supplies, and general support. After all, the claim had been made that it had been necessary to expel the Jews of Spain precisely because of the negative influence they had on the conversos, a factor supposedly responsible for their unsuccessful assimilation into Christian society; removing the Jews was the projected solution to the problem of judaizing.[68]

While the Jews were physically removed from the Spanish kingdom in 1492, the judaizing heresy was not as easy to dismiss. At the same time, the memory of past Jewish influence was to linger, as evidenced in confessions made before 1492, in trials held after 1492 that referred to pre-1492 contact and observance with Jews, and in the knowledge that had been acquired and perpetuated long after the demise of Spanish Jewry. As has been shown, these influences can be traced well into the sixteenth century.

On the other hand, after 1530, it was extremely rare to find a judaizer who had had contact with Jews or had experienced Judaism in his or her own lifetime. These trials are no longer those of relapsed heretics or of self-confessed judaizers who had neglected to tell the whole truth. These women were descendants of other conversas who had passed on their knowledge of Judaism, and had conveyed the importance of observing their ancestral religion to the best of their ability and knowledge.

Comparing the lives of judaizing women before and after 1492 leads to a rather startling discovery: as late as 1590, there was an unexpectedly high level of observance and awareness of Jewish law and practice in certain locales. One would imagine that a full century after the disappearance of the Jewish community, judaizing would diminish both in quantity and in quality. If the truth be told, after 1530, there was indeed a distinct decline in the numbers of trials of judaizers, both male and female; the Inquisition seemed to have been successful in its campaign to wipe out this heresy.[69] Yet the existence of strong crypto-Jewish communities such as that of Alcázar is impressive and thought-provoking. The Portuguese conversos who were destined to strengthen and re-awaken judaizing affinities in Spain in the late sixteenth and early seventeenth centuries had not yet reached these locales; the Jewish awareness and faith manifested here are none other than the organic products of Spanish crypto-Judaism itself.[70]

The element of continuity is, without a doubt, the most remarkable aspect of the lives of these judaizing women. The Jewish community, as influential as it was upon the crypto-Jews, had disappeared, yet judaizing survived the Expulsion. Despite the adversities, these women continued to transmit whatever knowledge of their heritage was in their possession. Some simply knew they should fast on Yom Kippur while others only learned to observe the Sabbath. At the same time, others succeeded in observing an impressive array of Jewish laws and rituals. Once the Inquisition was established, life for these crypto-Jewish women was a living hell; there was no safe place and no guarantee that one could even trust one's fellow judaizers. Yet they continued to observe and to teach their children and grandchildren; at their trials these crypto-Jewish women declared time and time again that whatever they had done had been in order to honor the Law of Moses and to attain salvation.

In the eyes of the Inquisition, the intention behind the deed was the crucial factor, and each and every judaizing act was a defiant example of heresy. While the earlier generations of judaizing women were aided and abetted by the Jewish community, the deeds and intentions of these conversas are surprisingly comparable both before and after the Expulsion. Although the fifteenth-century crypto-Jewish women clearly had a richer storehouse of Jewish source material, in the long run, their commitment and the consequences they faced did not differ from those of their sixteenth-century counterparts. The judaizing women of Castile were committed to their past and to its continuation; this was a serious commitment, for it was a matter of life and death.

NOTES

1. A detailed account of this occurrence is found in Yitzhak Baer, *A History of the Jews in Christian Spain* 2 (Phil.: *JPS,* 1962), 95-169; see also Haim Beinart, "The Great Conversion and the Converso Problem," *Moreshet Sepharad: The Sephardi Legacy* 1, ed. H. Beinart, (Jerusalem: Magnes Press, 1992), 346-382.

2. The controversy within Catholic ranks about how to deal with the conversos is discussed in Haim Beinart, *Conversos on Trial* (Jerusalem: Magnes Press, 1981), 1-20.

3. See, for example, the discussion of the Jewish life of the conversos of Ciudad Real in ibid., 237-285.

4. Responsa form the basis for the analysis of the conversos in B. Netanyahu, *The Marranos of Spain from the Late Fourteenth to the Early Sixteenth Century According to the Hebrew Sources* (New York: American Academy for Jewish Research, 1966). For a fine assessment of this work, see Gershon D. Cohen, "Review of B. Netanyahu's *The Marranos of Spain,*" *JSS* 29 (1967): 178-184.

5. The classic work on the Inquisition is that of Henry Charles Lea, *A History of the Inquisition of Spain,* 4 vols. (London: Macmillan and Co., Ltd., 1907). Among the more recent and worthy assessments of this institution are

Edward Peters, *Inquisition* (New York: Free Press, 1988) and William Monter, *Frontiers of Heresy* (New York: Cambridge University Press, 1990). For the most recent work on the events related to 1492, see Haim Beinart, *The Expulsion of the Jews from Spain* (Jerusalem: Magnes Press, 1994) (Hebrew).

6. For a brief analysis of the intrigues of conversos' servants and their masters and mistresses, see Renée Levine Melammed, "The Conversos of Cogolludo," *Proceedings of the Ninth World Congress of Jewish Studies* B, 1 (Jerusalem: World Union of Jewish Studies, 1986): 135-142.

7. For an analysis of this role as well as of the teaching methods of Castilian conversas, see Renée Levine Melammed, "The Ultimate Challenge: Safeguarding the Crypto-Judaic Heritage," *Proceedings of the American Academy for Jewish Research* 53 (1986): 93-109.

8. Beinart discusses the period of grace that took place in Ciudad Real in *Conversos*, 91-96.

9. The transcription of this trial, Legajo 143, número 11 (1483-4), appears in Haim Beinart, *Records of the Trials of the Spanish Inquisition in Ciudad Real* 1 (Jerusalem: Israel national Academy of Sciences and Humanities, 1974). The information to follow concerning María can be found on pp. 48-59. Hereafter legajo will be denoted as Leg., número as n°.

10. Leonor was tried separately, as recorded in Leg. 154, n° 22 (1484-92). This detail appears in ibid., 321.

11. This witness was Fernando de Trujillo; his testimony appears in ibid., 57-8.

12. These details can be found in the transcription of Leg. 164, n° 15 (1484-5); see ibid., 545-6. The mourning rites mentioned here as well as numerous others are discussed in Renée Levine Melammed, "Some Death and Mourning Customs of Castilian *Conversas*," *Exile and Diaspora* (Jerusalem: Ben-Zvi Institute, 1991), 157-167.

13. This information can be found in Leg. 133, n° 5 (1484-5) as transcribed in *Records* 1: 229-32.

14. Leg. 153, n° 10 (1487-94) is located in the Archivo Histórico Nacional, Madrid, under the category of Papeles de Inquisición de Toledo. In the arraignment, one of the charges referred to attending synagogue at the time of the Selihot services held in anticipation of the New Year. "Como se levantava muchas noches antes del ayuno mayor a medianoche poco mas o menos a rezar oraçiones judaycas e algunas dellas yva a la synoga a las rezar lo qual non hazia entre los judios salvo los que son mucho devotos."

In her confession, she explained: "Seyendo moça en casa de mi padre Gonçales, platero, vi a mi madre ayunar algunas vezes el ayuno mayor de la qual yo lo aprendi a fazer e ayunava el dicho ayuno yo entendia que me avia de saluar y creyendo ser ansi fue comienço...desde el dicho tienpo de my moçedad yo ayune algunas vezes el dicho ayuno mayor e otros ayunos de judios y los consenti ayunar a los de mi casa y algunas vezes antes que entrase el ayuno mayor me vañe e corte las uñas y en los tales dias vesti ropas linpias y estuve descalça...y ençendi candiles desde la tarde antes y demande perdon a otros e otros a mi e algunas noches antes del ayuno mayor fui a las xinogas a ver como ardian candiles y como rezavan los judios y les oya."

15. Beatriz's confession stated: "Digo my culpa que peque en guardar algunas pascuas de los judios con las çerimonias que ellos las guardavan las mas que yo podia y en espeçial la pascua del pan çençeno lo qual yo fazia e comia en mi casa e algunas vezes dava dello a algunos parientes y amigos y lo comieron en mi casa algunos dellos y algunas vezes lo compre e me lo presentava." However, when the charge was presented concerning "la vegilia de la pascua del pan çençeno," the prosecutor claimed that the defendant "començava a çenar en lechugas e apio con una salsa que los judios hasen para aquella noche." Ibid.

16. Beatriz confessed that "algunas vezes entre en las cavañuelas de los judios e comi en ellas de sus frutas." The prosecutor claimed, however, that she "hizo cabañuelas en su casa como judia pura." Ibid.

17. Two witnesses discussed this ritual, and its observance appears in a list of charges in Leg. 144, n° 3 (1491-2). The Jewish guest testified: "Dos vezes que pario su muger el dicho Alonso Lopes conbido este testigo e a su muger [Elvira] e dos veses la noche ante bautizarse e dezia: 'Mañana tengo de bautizar y deves folgar conmygo esta noche.' E yva alla e avya plaser e les dava fruta e se hazia como quando los judios hazen hadas a sus fijos."

For greater details on the *hadas*, see Renée Levine Melammed, "Noticias Sobre Los Ritos de Los Nacimientos y de la Pureza de la Judeo-Conversas Castellanas del Siglo XVI," *El Olivo* 8:29-30 (1989): 235-43.

18. In her trial, Leg. 160, n° 14 (1492-4), Elvira explained that the couple had "çiertos pares de casas e en algunas dellas moraron algunos judios, de los quales judios reçibimos algunos presentes, entre los quales presentes me enbiauan algunas veses tortas de pan çençeño, lo qual comiamos yo e mi marido e moças que avian en mi casa."

19. See Francisco Cantera Burgos and Carlos Carrete Parrondo, "Las Juderías Medievales en la Provincia de Guadalajara," *Sefarad* 34 (1974): 350.

20. See the list of charges in Leg. 177, n° 6 (1493).

21. See Leg. 181, n° 4 (1493-4).

22. See Leg. 178, n° 13 (1498-9).

23. The confession states "que en casa de my padre syendo de hedad de trese años poco mas o menos el dicho my padre que se llamava Diego Rodrigues, christiano nuevo, me dixo en dia de ayuno mayor de los judios: 'Fija, ayuna este dia y darte hija dios marido y darte fija muchos bienes.' Y este dicho dia una donsella que se llama Isabel de Cordova...me dixo asymysmo: 'Ven aca, hija, ayuna este ayuno y darte hija dios marido e muchos bienes.'" See Leg. 180, n° 10 (1498-9).

24. The following statement is recorded in the confession in ibid.: "Yten bien se me acuerda que preste a un judio una alcatifa e una savana orillada para faser su cabañuela qual todo yo fise por honrra e guarda de la ley de los judios

pensandome salvar por ella."

25. An analysis of this conversa's judaizing as well as of her husband's appears in Haim Beinart, "Judíos y Conversos en Casarrubios del Monte," *Homenaje a Juan Prado,* ed. L. Alvarez Verdes and E.J. Alonso Hernández (Madrid: Consejo Superior de Investigaciones Científicos, 1975), 645-57. The pertinent file is Leg. 154, n° 33 (1500). Here one can find the following confession by María concerning her observance of the purity laws: "Digo my culpa que guarde algunos veses quanto en my fue my purgaçion e despues al fyn me lavava algunas veses me vañava esto por çeremonia e algunas veses despues que paria a cabo de los syete dias me vestia ropas linpias e fasya echar savanas linpias en my cama porque me desya que era çeremonia."

26. See the accusation in Leg. 183, n° 11 (1502-3); the document states that Catalina "pedia e demando el pan çençeño a los judios e lo comya en la pascua dello por la honrrar e guardar."

27. See Leg. 158, n° 12 (1506-7).

28. This information appears in the accusation, confession as well as in her replies to the Inquisitors in Leg 160, n° 15 (1510-11). For example, when confronted with the fact that she had contact with Jews during Sukkot, she replied: "Es verdad...obe prestado ropas para las cabañuelas de los judios."

29. See the confession recorded in Leg. 152, n° 9 (1496).

30. The wife of Gómez Fernández de Castro confessed in Leg. 141, n° 13 (1511-13) as follows: "Un dia de los judios que me dixeron una my cuñada y suegra e dixeron que ayunase este dia e que todas las cosas que a dios demandase que el me las otorgaria e yo, señores, con ynocençia, ayune lo como ellas lo ayunava e en la noche demandeles perdon e ellas a mi."

31. This confession is found Leg. 169, n° 6 (1501).

32. Her extremely lengthy confession of fifteen years earlier included: "En el tal dia estava descalça e en pie e esta dia holga e no fasia fasienda alguna...e el dia antes me bañe lo mas secreto que podia...pedia perdon a algunas personas." She continued: "Que quando paria e me venya my regla apartava cama de my marydo y no tornava a su cama fasta que me bañava e estava linpia." See Leg. 150, n° 11 (1500-1).

33. Her confession of July 24, 1486, contains eighteen items. Her husband, Diego Rodríguez, also confessed on the same day to numerous judaizing acts. See Leg. 163, n° 7 (1512-22); note the lengthiness of this trial, which began twenty-six years after their confessions had been recorded.

34. María confessed to some forty sins of lesser and greater significance. For a full account, see Leg. 132, n° 8 (1500-1).

35. In the file of Aldonza de Herrera, Leg. 157, n° 2 (1530-1), the following statement appears on fols. 3v-4r: "Ynes Gonsales muger que fuy de Juan Espeçiero vesino de Cibdad de Toledo que moro en la colaçion de Sant Vicente parezco ante Vuestras Reverencias con gran dolor de mi anyma a dezir e magnifestar mys culpas e pecados quantos yo pecador he fecho e cometido en ofensa de Nuestro Señor Redentor Ihesu Christo e contra nuestra Santa Fe

Catholica faziendo algunas cerimonias judaycas pensando que era salvaçion a mi anima de los quales e de todos los que al presente a mi memoria ocurren con veriguencia grande dellos e con contriçion e arepentimiento de mi coraçon e con proposito de conplir la penitencia que por Vuestras Reverencias me saca inpuesta. Digo mi culpa: Primeramente Reverendo Padres digo que peque algunas vezes en guisar de comer el viernes para el sabado e lo comi y ençendi candiles los viernes en las noches por çerimonia. Peque en guardar algunos sabados e algunas pascuas de los judios y en los tales dias vesti ropas limpias por çerimonia. Peque en ayunar ayunos de judios fasta la noche espeçial el ayuno mayor que algunas vezes lo ayune y en tal dia pedi perdon a otros e otros a mi. Peque en comer algunas vezes pan çençeno en las pascuas de los judios quando ellos lo comen. Peque en comer carne degollada de mano de judío con cerimonia e quitar el sevo a la carne algunas vezes por çerimonia. Peque en dar limosna a judíos para azeite y en prestar algunas joyas para algunas fiestas de los judios. Peque que algunas vezes burlando o de veras dixe algunas palabras viçiosas tocante a Nuestra Santa Fe Catholica. Peque en que algunos dias de fiestas mandadas guardar por la madre Santa Yglesia los quebrante no guardandolos como era obligada. Peque en que algunos dias vedados por la Santa Madre Yglesia comy carne y leche e huevos defendido por ella. (4r) Peque que por muerte de algunos parientes mios comi en mesa baxa cosa de pescado e huevos e enbiar algunas vezes vianda para ello. Peque de que mys fijos e nietos me besavan la mano se la ponia en la cabeça en forma judayca. Peque en que algunas vezas estando mal mis fijos les eché algunas pastillas de azeite e los sahume. E porque ofendi a Nuestra Redentor e maestro Ihesu Christo en estas cerimonias de la ley de moysen e otras que al presente no son en my memoria protesto etcetera. En las quales cosas me inpuso my suegra Aldonça Gonsales difunta muger que fue de Francisco Gonsales sastre que biuia en la colaçion de Sant Vicente en el alhania los quales cosas ha veynte e cinco anos que fize fasta oy las quales dichas cosas fazia tanbien my marido. En tres de junio de LXXXV anos la dicha Ynes Gonsales presento esta confesion ante su Reverencia."

36. Teresa also mentioned in her first confession that she had begged a Jewish fellow to teach her to read, had learned a prayer and had observed some of the laws concerning the cleaning of meat. In 1493, she added that occasionally she had refrained from spinning on Friday nights, and that she had eaten a hen that had been slaughtered by a Jew. See Leg. 131, n° 5 (1493-4).

37. Leg. 133, n° 18 (1497-9) contains the following: "Dixo e confeso como despues de reconçiliada bolvyo ayunar e que ayuno el ayuno mayor de los judios non comyendo hasta la noche...Preguntada quantas veses avia ayunado el dicho ayuno mayor e quando, dixo que el año pasado lo ayuno e otras çinco o seys veses antes e que los avia ayunado con la misma yntençion y voluntad que de antes que se reconçiliase."

38. Mayor presented a very detailed confession in 1486; however, in 1500, she became involved in a messianic movement (which will be discussed below), and reverted to many of her former ways, even reciting part of a Hebrew prayer. See Leg. 155, n° 6 (1500-1).

39. Leg. 144, n° 4 (1503-4) contains information concerning three conversas, Elvira of Carrion, Juana de los Olivos of Ciudad Real, and Juana Ruíz. Juana Ruíz was reconciled after admitting to fasting in her father's home and observing the Sabbath. After being accused of judaizing again, she confessed; it is recorded that the defendant "dixo que es verdad que ella hiso todas las cosas contenydas en la dicha acusacion."

40. Her confession appears in Leg. 152, n° 10 (1513).

41. The prosecutor pointed to various days of fasting, "en espeçial el ayuno mayor e se hazia e haze en el mes de setienbre guardando en los tales dias de ayunos todas las çerimonyas segund costumbre de judios no comyendo en todo el dia fasta la noche y a la noche ella y otras personas que ayunavan los dichos ayunos çenavan carne e otras viandas a la judayca e se demandava perdon los unos a los otros como lo hazian los judios."

He then continued: "Despues de la dicha su reconçiliaçion a ayunado e ayuno los ayunos de los lunes e jueves entresemana como judia e al tienpo del verano y entreaño guardava e ayunava los ayunos otros de los judios." Ibid. Not only was she fasting on the traditional bi-weekly days of Monday and Thursday, but apparently fasted in the summer as well. These fasts most probably took place on the Ninth of Av and the Seventeenth of Tammuz.

42. This rich file is Leg. 152, no 15 (1530-1); the defendant was Mayor Gómez, widow of Diego de la Cuadra and then of Diego de Molina.

43. His confession appears in ibid., fol. 3v.

44. This confession follows immediately in ibid., fols. 4r-4v.

45. The statement made by this daughter, Aldonza Gómez, follows suit; see ibid., fol. 5r.

46. The next confession, that of Catalina, ibid., fols. 5v-6r, mentions "que alguna vezes rezava en un salterio."

47. Mayor stated that she judaized "hasta que me case con el dicho Diego de la Quadra my marido porque es buen Christiano nunca mas lo faze," ibid., fol. 6r.

48. See accusation in ibid., fols. 14r-v.

49. Her daughter Catalina appealed to the Court, stating that her mother was old and sick and that her life might be endangered. Ibid., fol. 25v. However, the Council voted for "tormento," ibid., fol. 26r. The torture, which is unexpectedly lengthy and cruel for this time period, is recorded on fols. 26v-28v.

50. The final decision stated that "fallamos el dicho promotor fiscal no aver provado su intencion tan complidamente quanto la devia provar para aver vitoria en esta causa," ibid., fol. 31r.

51. Haim Beinart has published a number of articles dealing with this phenomenon. See "The Spanish Inquisition and a 'Converso Community' in Extremadura," *Medieval Studies* 43 (1981): 445-71; idem, "Herrera: Its Conversos and Jews" (Hebrew), *Proceedings of the Seventh World Congress of Jewish Studies* B (Jerusalem: World Union of Jewish Studies, 1981), 53-85; idem, "The Prophetess Inés and Her Movement in Her Hometown, Herrera" (Hebrew), *Studies in Jewish Mysticism, Philosophy and Ethical Literature* (Jerusalem: Magnes Press, 1986), 459-506; idem, "A Prophesying Movement in Cordova in 1499-1502" (Hebrew), *Zion* 44 (1980): 190-200; idem, "The Prophetess Inés and Her Movement in Pueblo de Alcocer and Talarrubias" (Hebrew), *Tarbiz* 51 (1982): 633-58; idem, "Conversos of Chillón and the Prophecies of Mari Gómez and Inés, the Daughter of Juan Esteban" (Hebrew), *Zion* 48 (1983): 241-72.

52. Thirty-eight of these cases are analyzed in Renée C. Levine, *Women in Spanish Crypto-Judaism 1492-1520* (Ph. D. Dissertation, Brandeis University, 1983), 106-15. A fuller discussion of the conversas affected by this movement appears in a chapter in my forthcoming book to be published by Oxford University Press.

53. The arraignment in Leg. 172, n° 4 (1513-15) included the charge: "Iten que la dicha Leonor Nuñez con otras personas ayunaron el ayuno [mayor] de los judios que cabe en el mes de setienbre no comyendo en todo el dia fasta la noche y andavan descalços aquel dia visitandose de unas casas en otras donde se çelebrava e guardava el dicho dia e haziendo en el dicho dia las otras çerimonias que los judios acostubran hazer en los tales dias de ayunos judaycos."

54. The prosecutor was quite specific about her pretenses, claiming that she was not eating all day, "e despues a la noche çenando cosas vedadas a los catolicos christianos en los dias de ayunos...a algunos de los dichos dias de ayunos por disimular a los de casa hazia que comia sentandose a la mesa y la verdad era que no lo comia hasta la noche." See Leg. 151, n° 6 (1515-16).

55. The mother was María López, wife of Pedro de Villareal; her trial, Leg. 163, n° 8 (1516-21) began at the same time as her daughter's. The father was tried from 1518-21; see Leg. 188, n° 9. Isabel's trial, Leg. 162, n° 6 (1516-18), has been transcribed as a case study in Levine, *Women*, 339-404, and analyzed in terms of medieval justice in Renée Levine Melammed, "Sixteenth Century Justice in Action: The Case of Isabel López," *Revue des études juives* 145:1-2 (1986): 51-73.

56. For an analysis of these testimonies, see Levine Melammed, "The Conversos."

57. Leg. 134, n° 8 (1516-18) contains detailed descriptions of this widow's mourning observances. See Levine Melammed, "Some Death," 162-3 , n. 37; the clergyman's account can be found on p. 166, n. 48, and an additional account appears on pp. 166-7, n. 49.

58. Two of the prosecutor's charges pertain to observing this fast day; see Leg. 141, n° 16 (1518).

59. Leg. 158, n° 9 (1520-3) is replete with details of the life of a judaizing conversa. Isabel's rather unusual mourning rituals are analyzed in depth in Levine Melammed, "Some Death," 159, nn. 15-16; 163-5, n. 38; 40-44, 47.

60. The accusation that appears in Leg. 159, n° 15 (1520-1) is extremely lengthy and detailed, containing twelve counts. For example, the prosecutor even listed some of the ingredients included in Beatriz's Sabbath stew. On the other hand, when the defendant chose to confess, she denied any judaizing activities after her baptism; the Tribunal was, nevertheless, convinced by the prosecution, for the defendant was condemned to death.

61. Mayor was accused of having special places, both for the lighting of her Sabbath candles, and for isolating herself when she encountered the odor of pork products cooking. See Leg. 165, n° 7 (1520-1) and Carrete, "Guadalajara," 356.

62. This description is cited in Francisco Cantera Burgos and Carlos Carrete Parrondo, "La Judería de Hita," *Sefarad* 21 (1971): 264. The trial was recorded in Leg. 156, n° 9 (1538-9).

63. A look at the judaizing and in particular, at the prayers recited by this group of conversos appears in Renée Levine Melammed, "Judaizers and Prayer in Sixteenth Century Alcázar," *In Iberia and Beyond* (Delaware: University of Delaware Press, forthcoming). An analysis of testimonies of sisters and brothers that appear in these two files can be found in idem, "Women in (Post-1492) Spanish Crypto-Jewish Society," *Judaism* 41:2 (Spring, 1992): 156-168.

64. These details are provided during a session of questions and answers in 1590 in Toledo. See Leg. 138, n° 8 (1590-4), fols. 8v-11r. This is the trial of Juan del Campo, who is also mentioned by Isabel to have been a judaizer.

65. María requested to appear in order to confess; she was also interrogated in the hope of procuring additional details. These details appear in ibid., fols. 18r-22v; Juan del Campo, the defendant, is purported to have taught María's mother and to have read to her, along with engaging in other judaizing activities.

66. Catalina's confession is found in Leg. 187, n° 8 (1590-1), the trial of Francisco de Vega and his wife Ana del Campo. The confessant stated "que a guardado la ley de moysen y a guardado los sabados de sol a sol no travajando en ellos y a guardado los primeros dias de la luna y a guardado las tres pasquas del ano y que la una cayo par de la pasqua de Resurrecion y la otra a la pascua de mayo y la otra por el mes de septienbre a la feria de Alcaçar," fol. 7r; her statement continues on the following page.

67. Beatriz's relatively short statement appears in ibid., fols. 9r-9v.

68. The edict of expulsion itself makes this claim. For an English translation, see *The Expulsion 1492 Chronicles*, ed. David Raphael (No. hollywood, Calif.: Carmi House Press, 1992), 189-193. See too Beinart, "The

Expulsion from Spain: Causes and Results," *Moreshet Sepharad* 2, op. cit., 11-42.

69. See Monter, *Frontiers*, 53, for his chart on the stages of inquisitorial activity from 1480-1730.

70. For a discussion of these communities, see Beinart, "The Conversos in Spain and Portugal in the 16th to 18th Centuries," *Moreshet Sepharad* 2: 43-67.

Expulsion of the Jewish Community from the Spains, 1492

Lewis A. Tambs

Iberia and Sicily, both under Castilian and Aragonese rule in 1492, are the only areas in Western Europe where the three major revealed religions—Judaism, Christianity, and Islam—coexisted, clashed and contended for centuries.

Hebrews settled in Southern Iberia in Biblical Tharshish as well as in *Magna Graecia* in Sicily during Classical times. They were certainly rooted in Roman Baetecia—Andalusia—where they mingled with Iberians, Celts, Phoenicians, Greeks, Carthaginians, Romans and other migrants whom St. Paul aspired to evangelize.[1]

The Christian Church Council of Elvira (305) took note of Jewish presence by attempting to effect a separation between members of the two faiths. The submerging of Roman power and the Christian masses under waves of barbarian invaders crested with the Arian Visigoths in the fifth century. The Jewish community initially found favor with the heretical Visigoths who, like the Romans, strove for peninsular unity. However, with the conversion of King Reccared who sought unity through religion, the situation deteriorated. Persecution, in spite of papal denouncement of forced conversion, prevailed, especially after the Fourth Council of Toledo (633). Many migrated, but some 90,000 accepted baptism, some superficially, as pseudo-Christians, crypto-Jews or *Marranos*, others sincerely as New Christians.[2]

The Arab invaders of 711-718, which, according to tradition, included an African Jewish contingent, were abetted by dissident Christians and Jews. Conquered cities—Córdova, Málaga, Granada, Seville, and Toledo—were garrisoned by the Jewish inhabitants who were armed by the numerically few Arabs whose horsemen swept northward to central France only to be defeated at Tours in 732. As "People of the Book," Christians and Jews were granted religious liberty, which continued for both faiths under the early emirs. However, with the beginning of the Visigoth reconquest and the arrival in the emirate of intolerant Arab immigrants influenced by Caliph Harun-al Rashid (785-809) of Baghdad, whose reign coincided with the opening Saracen offensive against Sicily, and who persecuted Jew and Christian with equal vigor, Muslim tolerance for Spanish Christians eroded and by 850 martyrdom became common in the capital of Córdova. Meanwhile, Andalusian Jews engaged in medicine, agriculture, commerce, crafts, and in the silk and slave trades prospered, as did statesmen like Hasdai Ibn Shaprut and scholars under the Córdova Caliphs, especially Abd-Al-Rahman III (912-961).

Thus, by the tenth century Judaism received from Islam something more than persecution. Catching the contagion of Muslim poetry, philosophy, and science, a golden age dawned. The schismatic Quarites started a new Hebrew philology, which produced Qimhi; the gaon Saadiah founded a Jewish philosophy. Synagogue and secular poets like Ibn Gabriol and Halevi rose to prominence. The statesman Hasadi introduced a new spirit into Jewish culture which was noted for its comprehensiveness. Various expressions of human nature—literature, affairs, science, statecraft, and medicine—were harmoniously balanced, sometimes in an individual such as Maimonides, Moshe Ben Maimon (1135-1204)—physician, philosopher, and author of *Guide to the Perplexed* in which he attempted to reconcile Jewish dogma with Aristotle.

Córdova and Toledo served as centers of Arabic and Jewish culture and remained so even after the collapse of the Caliphate in 1031, when the Jews, caught on the losing side of a dynastic struggle for control of the Caliphate were briefly expelled. Others, however, superficially accepted Islam becoming crypto-Jews practicing Judaism in private while professing Mohammedanism in public.[3]

Some twelve petty *taifa* states replaced the Caliphate and Jews rose to high administrative positions in government, finance, commerce, and medicine. The Jews had a religious advantage over the Christians and the Muslims because in order to practice their faith properly they had to be able to read the sacred scriptures, an educational advantage confined to the monks and *Mullahs* who were isolated in monasteries and mosques. Thus, the other "People of the Book" were at a disadvantage until the reemergence of literate laymen which came with the revival of urban centers and commerce in western Europe—

especially northern Italy (Lombardy)—in the twelfth century. Hence, Jews served as tax farmers and tax collectors in southern Spain even after the arrival of the fanatical, warlike Almoravides in 1086, called to check the Christian Castilians who were advancing out of their northern mountain redout.[4]

Continuous conflict, constant casualties, and the extensive, unpopulated "no man's land" between Christian and Islamic Spain prompted Castile and León to revise their fifth column concept of Jews—the so-called Jewish betrayal of 711—and to welcome them as settlers with special status as the King's Jews. Active in commerce, and even as warriors and owners of estates, their numbers swelled in the twelfth century with the advent of the Almohades in Andalusia who practiced forced conversion, enslavement and destruction of temples. Even such scholars as Maimonides were forced to flee Córdova for Cairo.

The Reconquest paused after the Christian capture of Córdova and Seville in the mid-thirteenth century. Alfonso the Wise (1252-1284) in his legal code—*Las Siete Partidas*—accorded the Jews complete religious liberty (providing they did not attack the Christian faith or have authority over Christians) and endowed the *aljamas* with criminal and civil jurisdiction. Though defining the status of Jews and affirming their rights it did tend to reinforce segregation; *judios francos* (court Jews) were, however, allowed to live outside the community.[5]

Concurrently with the slackening of the Castilian reconquest in the south of the peninsula, Aragon extended its influence eastward to Sicily, which had been liberated by the Normans after nearly three centuries of Saracen rule. Advent of the Angevins eventually provoked an uprising and recognition of Aragonese suzereignty in the late thirteenth century. Initial Aragonese tolerance of the ancient, autocratic, artisan communities weakened with the introduction of Papal Inquisition in 1373 and the required wearing of a Jewish badge. In contrast to the community in Sicily, Peninsular Jews fared quite well into the late fourteenth century.[6]

Prosperity earned from finance, tax farming, land leasing, money lending, trade and commerce capped by high positions at Court provoked a popular reaction, ignited, in part, by outside events. With the advent of the Lombards, Edward I of England found the Jews redundant and expelled them in 1290; Philip IV of France banished both the Jews and the Lombards in 1306. He then crushed and beggared the Templars—the international financiers of the day—the following year. The Jews, briefly recalled, were again banished in 1394.

The Sephardic communities in Bayonne and Bordeaux were, however, tolerated. Not until Oliver Cromwell—three and a half centuries later—did a covert return commence in England. Full parliamentary rights were not granted until 1858-1860. France waited until the Revolution—some four centuries.

Many of these exiles, particularly the French, sought refuge in Castile. But dark days were ahead. Caught supporting the losing side in a dynastic civil war between Henry of Trastamara and Peter the Cruel, they were shorn of the royal shield. Under popular pressure incited by the sermons of Ferrant Martínez as well as conversos like Pablo de Santamaría and Geronimo de Santa Fé, mob violence on the juderías erupted in 1391 in Seville, Córdova, Toledo, Messina and other cities. Mayhem, murder, and mass conversions followed. Tranquility returned, but St. Vincent Ferrer, who personally opposed forced conversion, touched off another wave of baptisms of tens of thousands. Entire communities, perhaps even more than had deserted Judaism during the sojourn in Egypt in the fourteenth century B.C.E., apostatized.[7] Safety and salvation may have been paramount, but, perhaps, many of these New Christians may have converted to Christianity en masse circa 1400 in part out of an intense desire to participate actively and energetically, on a more direct and equal basis, in the Christian effort to destroy the last vestige of Islamic power in the Iberian Peninsula.[8] The Muslim Nasrid Kingdom of Granada practiced enslavement, persecution, deportation, and disdain of the Jews.

Now that the partial integration had been achieved, the Crown's problem was not open adherence to Judaism—repressive measures were abrogated (1419-1420), and religious services were legal until 1492—but Marranism or crypto-Judaism, Jews who covertly kept their faith while enjoying the rights and privileges of Christians. "They were Jews in all but name, and Christians in nothing but form."[9] These crypto-Jews should be distinguished from New Christians, most of whom were sincere. Many New Christians came from the affluent, educated, urban class, and rose to the highest positions in the Court, Church, and commerce. Moreover, many of the oldest and exalted, but impoverished hidalgo families grafted Jewish wealth, talent and learning to their family trees to the extent that in Aragon, an estimated one-third of the nobility were of Jewish descent.[10]

Corruption and chaos claimed Castile during most of the fifteenth century. Robber barons, dynastic wars, and inept monarchs reigned. The community, mostly relegated to rural areas, was relatively secure until past mid-century when popular sentiment against New Christian tax farmers, inflamed by the *converso* Alfonso de Spina, ignited attacks on the *aljamas*. Even the nobility which had favored conversion and intermarried with the New Christians was shaken when "at the Cortes of Fraga (1460) large numbers of *conversos* attended much to the dismay of the *hidalgos*."[11] Restrictions were reimposed but chaos continued until the ascension to the thrones of the dual monarchy, Isabel to Castile (1473), and Ferdinand to Aragon (1479). They imposed order and welcomed the Genoese.

> The Ligurian population of Seville had been small during the fourteenth and fifteenth centuries, but in the second half of the fifteenth it experienced steady growth. Civil strife with the Ligurian Republic, the gradual loss of her eastern colonies to the Turks, and the opening of Africa by the Portuguese attracted numerous representatives of the great commercial families of Genoa to Seville. Between 1450 and 1500 the Genoese population of the city doubled.[12]

Jews, nevertheless occupied powerful posts in Castile. Most notable was Abraham Senior "who administered the indirect taxes of the Kingdom of Castile for many years . . . and to whom Isabel granted a life annuity of 150,000 *maravedis* in appreciation for his assistance to her husband in mounting the throne."[13] Also of note was R. Isaac Abravanel, philosopher, scholar, and tax farmer in central and southern Castile, who served as the Queen's private business and financial agent, and who extended vast loans to the Crown for the coming Crusade against Granada.[14]

New Christians were more than prominent in the palace. The Heronymite, Hernándo de Talavera, Tomás de Torquemada's successor, as Isabel's confessor, was later her appointee as Bishop of Granada. Two other New Christians of note were Luís de Santángel, Keeper of the Queen's Privy Purse, and Pedro de Caballería, a court confidant. Even Tomás de Torquemada, the Queen's confessor while she was still Infanta and the future Grand Inquisitor was allegedly of Jewish ancestry. The same is said of Ferdinand of Aragon.[15]

The Jewish and the New Christian community, though challenged commercially by the Genoese, enjoyed royal favor. The royal pair, however, were determined to forge geographical and religious unity.

Islamic Granada, a tributary of Castile, hastened both trends— geographic and religious—in 1476, when Muley-Abu-l-Hasan, accustomed to defying Isabel's successor, Enrique IV, taunted the Castilian ambassador's demand for payment with: "Tell your monarch that the Kings of Granada who paid tribute are dead; our mint now coins only blades of scimitars and heads of lances."[16] Isabel, who was still organizing Castile, and Ferdinand, who had not yet ascended to the Aragonese throne, but whose realm did include Sardinia and Sicily, were not immediately up to the task of the Granadine challenge. Religious homogeneity came first.

In 1478, Pope Sixtus IV granted the Castilian Crown the right to establish a Royal Inquisition. In an effort to pursue persuasion, Isabel dispatched a pious prelate to Seville, the center of Marranist activity, to investigate Jews who masqueraded as Christians or Jews who sought to reconvert New Christians; both acts were civil offenses. The results were inconclusive and formal foundation of the Inquisition followed in 1480.

The Court of the Holy Office began operations in Andalusia—site of the greatest Marranist activity and the base of operations for the impending Granada Campaign—Seville in 1481, Córdova, a year later, and Ciudad Real—later transferred to Toledo—in 1483.[17]

> The records of the Court speak for themselves as they describe how a flourishing *Converso* community in fifteenth-century Spain was demolished by the Inquisition. From them we get a comprehensive picture of life in that community and of the relations of its members to both Judaism and Christianity. For, when stripped of its outer mantle of Christianity, the *Converso* community of Ciudad Real emerges as an essentially Jewish community.[18]

After the arrival of the Inquisitors and establishment of the Court, an Edict proclaimed a Period of Grace (forty to one hundred and thirty days depending on the locale) for confession and reconciliation. This Period of Grace enabled the Inquisitors to collect evidence, to learn to distinguish local gossip from fact, and to open trials as well as to allow those who erred to confess. Those who confessed and informed on others were promised absolution. Old Christians and *conversos* informed on their New Christian neighbors. "All family ties were broken and no allegiances were honored."[19]

In Seville the upper class initially greeted the Holy Office with jealousy and suspicion for many had married wealthy Jewesses. However, as *auto-de-fes* against crypto-Jews commenced—Jews were obliged to testify against their covert co-religionists—the community in

Seville reacted with an ill-fated plot of armed rebellion which, upon discovery, quickened the tempo of the Court.[20]

Isabel did, however, make one last effort to compromise and win over the Jews to Christianity by commanding the publication of a simple catechism, but to no avail. Scores, hundreds, perhaps thousands, were executed. The exact number is difficult to ascertain due to incomplete documentation and the Inquisition's habit of simulating execution of escaped fugitives as well as burning effigies of the deceased.

A more precise figure is available for the years 1540-1700 when the Inquisition tried some 100,000 cases, not necessarily concerning crypto-Jews, many not for heresy or sedition but on lesser charges such as blasphemy, fornication outside of marriage, etc. During the one-hundred-sixty year period 828 were executed or relaxed to the secular arm.[21]

> While we today rightly decry such executions, we should also realize that given the mentality of the times, that number was somewhat low. Actually the Spanish compared quite "favorably" in the number of Catholics executed in Protestant England during the same era.

> By the end of the reign of Elizabeth I (1559-1603), as many as 250 Catholics had been executed by the English government for their faith [not to mention other Dissenters] (about eighty were tortured before execution), the majority being priests. The whole Spanish empire—Spain itself and its overseas possessions—had a lower number of executions during this period. Not all of them were related to religion; crimes against the state were also included.[22]

Queen Elizabeth's successors, the Stuarts, continued her campaign against dissenters. Irish recusants rose in 1641. Civil War erupted the next year. The coming to power of the Protector Oliver Cromwell initiated a decade of intolerance, repression, and genocide, particularly in Ireland. Between 1642 and 1652, three bishops and more than 300 priests were martyred. Thousands of men, women, and children were sold as slaves in the West Indies and the population of Ireland reportedly declined by over 800,000 through exile, starvation, and slaughter. Not until 1829, some thirty years before their Jewish compatriots, did the Catholic Emancipation Act pass Parliament. Thus, tragically, prejudice, persecution, and martyrdom were not confined to the Spains.[23]

The Courts of the Inquisition continued apace in the 1480s. Many Jews and New Christians were tried. Many Spanish Jews and New Christians were also reconciled. However, since it was believed the Jews were not only causing *conversos* to relapse, but that they were allies and informers of the Muslims, with the opening of the final offensive against Granada, expulsion from Adalusia was decreed in 1483. Rodrígo Ponce de León, Duke of Cádiz, principal commander of the Granada campaign carried out the orders. The same year, the Dominican Torquemada was designated the Grand Inquisitor of Castile. He quickly stepped up the pace against the crypto-Jews and crypto-Muslims and assorted Christian heretics.

The Holy Office, over stiff opposition, was introduced into Aragon in 1484. The New Christians countered with a successful conspiracy to kill the Inquisitor, St. Pedro Arbues, whose murder provoked a violent popular reaction against the *juderías*. Meanwhile, the Granada campaign ground on, but time was running out for the community. The *coup de grace* came with charges of ritual child murder (the La Guardia case of 1488-1491) and the winning of geographical unity with the gaining of Granada in January 1492.[24]

On March 31, 1492 Ferdinand and Isabel signed at Aljambra, but did not promulgate, the Edict expelling all members of the Jewish religion.[25] Until enforcement of the Edict it remained legal to openly practice Judaism throughout the Spains.

> . . . it is well known or should be known that there are in these kingdoms some bad Christians who follow Jewish ways and apostatize our Holy Catholic Faith. This great harm is caused by intercourse of Christians with Jews. . . . In the *Cortes* (Parliament) of Toledo in 1480 we commanded that said Jews be segregated in all cities, towns, and hamlets in all our Kingdoms and Seigniories and gave them *juderías* (*aljamas* or Ghettos) and places apart. . . .

> We ordered the establishment of the Inquisition some twelve years ago. The Inquisitors have found, we are informed, many guilty religious, ecclesiastical and secular persons who have caused great harm to Christians because of their intercourse, communication and conversation with Jews who attempt thru various means and manners to subvert and humiliate our Holy Catholic Faith and separate faithful Christians from it by preaching

and proselytizing their harmful beliefs and opinions and instructing them in ceremonies and observances of their laws.

. . . In order to stop such intercourse we ordered (in 1483) that all such persons depart Andalusia where it appeared they had done the greatest harm, believing that (such segregation) would be enough in cities, towns, and places in Our Kingdoms and Seigniories and that they would cease to commit said acts. We have, however, been informed that in spite of justice administered to some of the Jews that they have continued to commit such crimes and offenses against Our Holy Catholic Faith. . . . Therefore, after due consideration, council and deliberation we banish all Jews and Jewesses dwelling within the confines of Our Kingdoms, never to return. . . . They must depart no later than the end of July of this present year with all their children, servants, and relatives, adults and minors of all ages.

. . . In order that the Jews may settle their affairs. . . . We guarantee them Our Royal protection, as well as the security of their lives and possessions, until the end of July. . . . We grant them permission and license to remove by land and sea from all Our Kingdoms and Seigniories their goods and properties with the exception of gold, silver, and minted coins or other objects that fall under existing prohibitions. . . .[26]

The thrust of the Expulsion Edict has been described as:

. . . a curious blend of racial and religious motives. Ostensibly, the whole purpose of the Expulsion was to excise from the body politic a foreign racial element which the Spanish Christians were unable to assimilate. In fact, however, this Expulsion, like others in the Middle Ages, was a means of religious coercion. The Catholic Monarchs did not employ cruel and shocking measures to force Christianity upon the Jews, as was done in Portugal a few years later; but they helped to facilitate conversion. Simultaneously with the Edict of Expulsion, they enacted certain laws for the benefit of the converts, promising such persons aid and protection and exempting them for a time from the control of the Inquisition so as to allow them leisure to accustom themselves to their new faith.[27]

Thus, the tenor of the Expulsion Edict appears to be more religious than racist—particularly so since a great deal of intermarriage had occurred and Jews were held in high esteem by Ferdinand and Isabel.

The royal pair were reportedly offered a fortune on March 31, 1492 at the Hall of the Ambassadors in the Aljambra by Senior and Abravanel not to sign the Expulsion Edict. But legend has it they were frustrated by the sudden intrusion of Torquemada, who allegedly threw "a crucifix on the table shouting that they were betraying Christ for 30,000 pieces of silver as Judas did for 30. . . ."[28] One, Abraham Senior, would convert to Christianity. The other, Isaac Abravanel, would remain with the faith of his fathers. He would, however, enjoy some royal favor to the end being "granted a special permit to take one thousand gold ducats and various gold and silver ornaments out of the country."[29]

In the month intervening between the signing of the Edict and publication, Isabel replaced her New Christian confessor, Talavera, whom she designated Bishop of Granada, with Francisco Ximenez de Cisneros, who would aid her in reforming the Spanish Church, publish the *Polyglot Bible*, and eventually serve as Regent and Grand Inquisitor. Isabel and Ferdinand also signed the Capitulation of Santa Fé commissioning Christopher Columbus' voyage of discovery, designating him Admiral of the Ocean Sea and patenting him Viceroy of lands which he may discover. Funding came from Luís Santángel, Keeper of the Queen's Privy Purse, who collaborated with Francisco Pinelo, a Genoese merchant, and resident of Seville, who loaned 1,400,000 *maravedis* for the voyage. Santángel, grandson of a *converso*, was implicated but not charged in the crypto-Jewish conspiracy which culminated in the assassination of the Aragonese Inquisitor St. Pedro Arbues in Saragossa in 1485. Santángel also proposed that the recently fined port of Palos be required to supply two ships in exchange for cash. A suggestion which helped launch Columbus on his Great Enterprise to the Indies.[30]

Meanwhile, promulgation of the Edict was pending. The community, however, had some forewarning since a month elapsed between signing and proclamation.

Publication of the Edict obliged the Jews:

> to dispose of all their property that was not portable in three months. [They] were virtually at the mercy of their purchases. . . hence a Jew would give a house for an ass and a vineyard for a tapestry or a piece of linen.[31]

Some swallowed gold ducats, others allegedly used letters of credit, but even with this and the silks and skins exported the loss of wealth was incalculable. Many converted to save themselves, their families and their inheritance.[32]

The number who trudged in painful procession toward the ports or neighboring nations has been estimated between 70,000 to 800,000. Modern scholarship seems to have settled on something between 100,000 and 165,000 Sephardi who departed out of an estimated Jewish population of possibly 300,000 and a New Christian contingent of up to 700,000.[33] It was a tragic finale to a splendid history for "Spanish Jews were the greatest luminaries of Hebrew civilization since Biblical times."[34]

Given this unfortunate end to a glorious past, one must ask why?

Many motives may have contributed to the decision to issue the Edict of Expulsion—religious fervor; a desire to defend the Faith against apostasy and heresy; determination to unite Iberia through religion in the Roman and Visigoth tradition; fear of the Jews as a Fifth Column in the face of the ever present Moorish menace; *converso* animosity toward their former co-religionists; Genoese commercial competition; and greed for Jewish gold on the part of the Crown. All of these, with the possible exception of the last (although some individuals and institutions did profit from the Expulsion, the royal pair was well aware that revenue from Andalusia had declined after the Expulsion in 1483) were probably contributing factors.[35]

However, government, as St. Thomas Aquinas emphasizes, exists primarily to dispense justice.[36] Certainly some Jews sought to reconvert their separated brethren. "Certainly, not all those expelled were innocent. But the majority, comprising most of the women and all of the children, must have been."[37] Hence, of all the glories of the reign of Ferdinand and Isabel, the Expulsion stands out as a stain on their shield—an act of injustice.

European reaction to promulgation of the Expulsion Edict was favorable for religious and *real politic* reasons. Pico de la Mirandola reflected one, Nicolo Machiavelli, the other.[38] Even Sultan Bayazid III welcomed the news, as he did the refugees, chiding Ferdinand, "Do not you call this King a statesman, who impoverishes his land and enriches mine?"[39] For many of the exiles, no matter their initial destination—Portugal, Navarre, France or Italy—eventually migrated to Ottoman domains, where they served the Sultan, as did the Armenians, in administration, finance, and commerce. Both of these minorities would be victims of genocide in the progressive, forward-looking, rational and scientific twentieth century.[40] In 1492, however, the Ottoman menace still stirred.

In mid-May Muslim mounted patrols probed the Austrian Alps in Carpathia and Styria. Almost unchecked, except by the Serbs, the Ottomans had advanced out of the east for over two centuries, overrunning the Balkans, conquering Constantinople, and challenging Venice in the Aegean and the Adriatic. The tempo quickened in 1480 with the occupation of Otranto while from 1483 forward the shores of Spain were savaged in support of the Saracens in Granada. These Muslim moves against Aragonese coasts in Italy and Iberia had not only hampered operations against Granada but were welcomed by the Saracens of Spain and North Africa.[41]

With the fall of Granada, Fez openly allied itself with Sultan Bayazid III and his successors. Ottoman military might moved westward on land and sea until checked by the heirs of Ferdinand and Isabel at Vienna in 1529 and again in 1683, (the Jews had been expelled earlier in 1670), and at Lepanto in 1571. At Lepanto, the largest naval battle since Actium, the Spanish fleet aided by papal and Venetian squadrons shielded Christendom. Lepanto stymied the generalized Ottoman assault in the Eastern Mediterranean which seized Cyprus. Lepanto also coincided with the revolt of the Moriscos (converted Spanish Muslims suspected of retaining their original faith) which led to their final expulsion in 1609.[42] Hence, both Marranos and Moors suffered the same fate. In both of these cases of intolerance, the Crown exercised three of the four options open for resolving minority problems: segregation (*juderías, aljamas, morerías*); integration (conversion); and transportation (expulsion; Jews, 1492; Moriscos, 1609); leaving the fourth, liquidation (holocaust, ethnic cleansing), for more modern Europeans.[43]

The immense human tragedy of the Expulsion of the Jews from Castile and Aragon often overshadows the great cultural contributions by *marranos* and New Christians both prior to and after 1492. As the Sephardi prepared for either forced exile or integration, Don Abraham Senior and his son-in-law, R. Meir Malamed, were baptized at Santa María de Guadalupe. Senior, treasurer-general of the Holy Brotherhood (*Santa Hermandad*) and lessee of most of Castile, served as the last Jewish court-appointed rabbi of Castile. Sponsored by the King, Queen and Cardinal Archbishop González de Mendoza of Toledo the pair took the names of Fernándo Nuñez Coronel and Fernándo Pérez Coronel. This distinguished Catholic family was among the many New Christians such as Fernándo de Rojas, author of the first Castilian novel

La Celestina; Juan Luís Vives, Christian Humanist and Catholic Apologist; Luís de León, theologian and poet; Juan de Polanco, secretary to St. Ignatius Loyola, Vicar General of the Society of Jesus, and assistant to St. Francis Borgia at the Council of Trent; and quite possibly Diego Lainez, second General of the Jesuits, St. John of the Cross, and St. Teresa of Avila, who contributed to the literary and religious Golden Age of Spain.[44]

The deadline arrived and the wretched refugees set sail. On August third Columbus also weighed anchor at Palos. As the morning ebb tide carried the *Santa María, Niña,* and *Pinta* down the Río Tinto, over the bar of the Río Saltés and out into the open Atlantic, legend has it that the seamen could see the sails of the exiles in the distance as they stood for North Africa. Aboard the Admiral's flagship stood the expedition's recently baptized interpreter, Luís de Torres, whose fluency in Hebrew and Arabic would be essential when Columbus made landfall in the empire of the Great Khan. Torres would later be granted extensive estates in Cuba and is credited with introducing American tobacco to Europe.[45]

Three days after the last of the banished bravely faced a hostile world and Columbus departed Palos, an enclave convened in Rome to elect a new pope. The cardinals chose the Valencian Rodrigo Borgia as the successor of St. Peter. Isabel was not pleased, having favored the candidacy of Cardinal González de Mendoza of Toledo.

Taking the name of Alexander VI, this corporally corrupt Catalan but theologically orthodox pontiff:

> was the first sovereign to open to the Jews the harbors of papal territory. Against the will of the local Roman Jews he accorded the exiled Spaniards extensive hospitality. It was his example only which burst the iron ring of coasts and now Naples and Venice also granted them shelter.[46]

Thus, those banished from Barcelona and Valencia found refuge in the papal states while the exiles from Sardinia and Sicily where mass conversions had earlier occurred were welcomed in Naples.

Later in August as the refugees sought shelter, Antonio de Nebrija published his *Gramática de la Lengua Castellana* at Salamanca. Written with the Queen's encouragement and dedicated to her this work marked "the transition of Castilian from the status of a vernacular language to that of a cultivated one.[47] This grammar, the first Romance language to be standardized, served as the literary base of

Roja's novel *La Celestina,* published some years later, and would form the basis for imperial linguistic unity in the Peninsula, Africa, the Americas, and the Pacific, much the same as Spanish Catholicism did for religious or ideological uniformity.

Religious and linguistic unity would gather together the far flung geographically distant and ethnically diverse global empire which would endure for over three centuries. Nevertheless, the cost was high. Though *conversos* and New Christians would contribute mightily to the Golden Age of art, literature, empire, and Counter Reformation; and though clandestine communication would continue for centuries, the Sephardi were banished unjustly from hearth and homeland.

Not until the nineteenth century, though some synagogues were briefly opened in the 1700s, were amends initiated. In 1834 the Inquisition was abolished for the third and last time. In 1868 the Expulsion Edict of 1492 was briefly softened during the interregnum between Isabel II and Amadeo I. The next year, Article XI of the Constitution of 1869, though declaring Catholicism the state religion, further stated:

> the exercise of in private or public of any other religion is guaranteed to all foreigners resident in Spain without any further limitation than the universal rules of Morality of Law (Jews were included in that category of foreigners).[48]

After the Restoration, Madrid welcomed Jewish refugees from Russia in 1882. Then in December 1924, the Government of General Miguel Primo de Rivera proclaimed that "all individuals of Spanish origin," including Sephardim, could acquire full civil and political rights by presenting credentials at the nearest Spanish Consulate—a decree which enabled Spain to give safe passage and protection to some Jewish refugees during World War II. However, it was not until 1965 when Generalissimo Francisco Franco (whom some Jews and many Spaniards believed was of Sephardic stock) proclaimed religious toleration in the *Fuero de los Españoles* followed by implied revocation of the Expulsion Edict on December 13, 1968, that Jews were legally permitted to freely practice their faith.[49] Culmination came on the five hundred year anniversary of the Edict's signing—March 31, 1992—when King Juan Carlos and Queen Sophia:

> and the president of Israel, Chaim Herzog, symbolically stanched this historic wound in a Madrid synagogue in the

course of an extraordinary ceremony, [which] as the king said, was particularly precious to the Crown, since it marked the meeting of the Spanish Jews or residents with their King and Queen. . . . It was also a token of recognition of the "fortitude of spirit and ability to preserve their cultural roots shown by the Hispano-Jews" or Sephardim, who have kept alive up to the present time the language and customs of Sepharad, the old Hebrew name for Spain.

For his part, the Israeli president said: "This is a very moving occasion, which will be remembered by our respective people as a historic reconciliation between the Jewish people and the people of Spain." The essence of the ceremony, which was attended by many Spanish and Jewish personalities, was summed up by His Majesty King Juan Carlos in his speech: "Sepharad is no longer a sense of yearning, but a homeland where it should not be said that Jews are to feel at home, because Hispano-Jews are at home."

"What matters now is not to draw up lists of mistakes or successes," but to "analyze the past in light of our future," the King added.[50]

For the Sephardi had remained Castilian and Catalan to the core for five centuries, carrying their language, culture, music, and art with them to distant lands and far away places. Exiles all, surrounded by foreign languages, foods, customs, climes, and conventions, they had carried their Hispanic homeland in their hearts. Now, in 1992, the community, after half a millennium of exile, was home—at last.

NOTES

I would like to extend my thanks to Ms. Carolyn Heath, Mr. Robert Bromberg and Mr. James Dybdahl for their help in preparing this paper.

1. Romans, XV, 22, 25; and Cecil Roth, *History of the Jews in Italy* (Philadelphia: Jewish Publication Society of America, 5701-1946), 1-5.
2. "Spain," *Jewish Encyclopedia* 11 (New York: KTAV, 1964): 485; "Spain," *Encyclopedia Judaica* 15 (New York: Macmillan, 1971): 222; José Amador de los Rios, *Historiá Social, Política, Relgiosa de los Judíos de España y Portugal* 2

(Buenos Aires: Bajel, 1943): 387-9; Christopher Hare, *A Queen of Spain* (New York: Harper, 1900), 212.

3. Amador de los Rios, *Judíos* 1:62-85; "St. Eulogius," *Lives of the Saints*, Augustine Kalberer, ed. (Chicago: Franciscan-Herald, 1983), 88-9; "Sts. Flora and Mary," Ibid., 429-300; "Jews" *Encyclopedia Britannica, 11th Edition* 15 (Cambridge: U.K.: University Press, 1911): 404; and Chaim Raphael, *Road from Babylon* (London: Weidenfeld & Nicolson, 1985), 67-82.

4. *Encyclopedia Judaica* 15:226-38; Américo Castro, *Structure of Spanish History*, trans. Edmund King (Princeton, N.J.: Princeton, 1954), 470; Nissim Elnecave (sefa 'tah) *Los hijos de Iberia-Franconia* (Buenos Aires: La Luz, 1981), 85-90; interview with Sol Sanders, 18 Nov. '92.

5. Ibid.; *Encyclopedia Judaica* 15:231-38; and Israel Abram, *Jewish Life in the Middle Ages* (Antheneum, N.Y.: Temple, 1978), 50.

6. Roth, *Jews in Italy*, 246-8; and Moses Shalvass, *Jews in the World of the Renaissance*, trans. Elvin I. Kose (Leiden: Brill & Spertas College of Judaica Press, 1973), 26-7.

7. Amador de los Rios, *Judíos* 1:566-668; Yitzhak Baer, *History of the Jews in Christian Spain* 2 (Philadelphia: Jewish Publication Society, 1966-5726):95-169; Castro, *Structure*, 507; Haim Beinart, *Conversos on Trial* (Jerusalem: Magnes, 1981), 1-9; *Jewish Encyclopedia* 11:497; Mair José Bernadete, *Hispanic Culture and Character of Sephardic Jews* (New York: Hispanic Institute, 1953), 27-33; Cecil Roth, *History of the Marranos* (New York: Harper & Row, 1966), 14-20; and Roth, *Jews*, 246-8.

8. Allan Harris Cutler and Helen Elmquist Cutler, *Jews as the Ally of the Muslim* (Notre Dame, Indiana: Notre Dame, 1986), 312.

9. Roth, *Marranos,* 20.

10. Nicolás López Martínez, *Los judaizantes castellanos y la Inquisición en el tiempo de Israel la Católica* (Burgos: Semenario Metropolitano de Burgos, 1954), 56-74, 104-14; Amador de los Rios, *Judíos* 2:5-78; Julio Caro Baroja, *Los judíos en la España moderna y contemporanea* (Madrid: Arion, 1961), 65-82; Carols Carrete Parrondo, "Fraternization Between Jews and Christians in Spain Before 1492," *American Sephardi* 9 (1978): 15; Philip Wayne Powell, *Tree of Hate* (Vallecito, Calif.: Ross House, 1985), 50-70; and Beinart, *Conversos,* 25-43.

11. "Spain," *Jewish Encyclopedia* 11:500.

12. Ruth Pike, *Enterprise & Adventure: Genoese Traders in Seville* (Ithaca, NY: Cornell, 1966), 1; see Felipe Fernández-Armesto, *Canary Islands After the Conquest* (Oxford: Clarendon, 1982), 22-5; and Richard Henry Boulind, "The Strength and Weakness of Spanish Control of the Caribbean, 1520-1650," (Ph.D. dissertation, University of Cambridge, 1965), 169 for Genoese commercial activities.

13. Baer, *Jews* 2:315.

14. Ibid., 318-19; Thomas Hope, *Torquemada: Scourge of the Jews* (London: George Allen and Unwin, 1939), 204-5; and Alexander Marx, *Studies in Jewish History and Booklore* (New York: Jewish Theological Seminary, 5704-1944), 91-93.

15. Baer, *Jews*, 433-5; Rafael Sabatini, *Torquemada and the Spanish Inquisition* (Boston and New York: Houghton Mifflin, 1924), 91, note 1; John E. Longhurst, *Age of Torquemada*, 2nd ed. (Lawrence, Kansas: Coronado, 1961), 41; Cecil Roth, *Spanish Inquisition* (New York: Norton, 1964), 41; Henry C. Lea, *Inquisition of Spain* 1 (New York: Macmillan, 1906): 120; Roth, *Marranos*, 39; Hope, *Torquemada*, 18-19; William Thomas Walsh, *Characters of the Inquisition* (Rockford, IL: Tan, 1987), 131-2; Marx, *Studies in Jewish History*, 103; Jerne L. Plunket, *Isabel of Castile* (New York: Putman, 1919/1968), 258-9; José Faur, *In the Shadow of History, Jews and Conversos at the Dawn of Modernity* (Albany, NY: State University of New York, 1992), 44-5; Hare, *Queen*, 239; and Harry S. May, *Francisco Franco: The Jewish Connection* (Washington, DC: University Press of America, 1978), 72, 92, footnote no. 24.

16. Ibid., 114.

17. Haim Beinart, *Records of the Trials of the Spanish Inquisitor in Ciudad Real* 1 (Jerusalem: Israel National Academy of Sciences and Humanities, 1974): xiii-xxi.

18. Ibid., 1:xiii.

19. Ibid., 1:xvii.

20. Hare, *Queen*, 206-14.

21. "Spain," *Jewish Encyclopedia* 11:500; Roth, *Marranos*, 34; W.T. Waugh, *History of Europe*, 3rd ed. (London: Methuen, 1932), 352-465; Henry Kamen, *Spain: 1469-1714*, 2nd ed. (London and New York: Longman, 1991), 38-44; Amador de los Rios, *Judíos* 2:191-220; López Martínez, *Judaizantes*, 187-252; Hope, *Torquemada*, 18-23, 197-200; "Inquisition," *Jewish Encyclopedia*, 6:587-593; Haim Beinart, "La inquisición española y la expulsión de los Judíos de Andalucía," *Jews and Conversos*, ed. Yoset Kaplan (Jerusalem: Magnes, 1981), 103-123; Elkan Nathan Adler, *Auto de Fé and the Jew* (London: Oxford, 1908), 53, 106-107; Rafael García Boix, *Autos de Fé y las causas de la Inquisición de Córdoba* (Córdoba: Diputación Provincial, 1983), 1-6; and Bienart, *Records of the Trials* 1:xiii-xxxiv; and Raphael, *Babylon*, 107-113.

22. Fr. Benjamin Luther, "The Church and the Spanish Inquisition," *Miles Jesu*, 20, no. 2 (Feb. 1995): 8.

23. William Petty, *Political Anatomy of Ireland* (Dublin: A. Thomas, 1869), 187; and see Myles O'Reilly, *Memorials of Those Who Suffered for the Catholic Faith in Ireland* (New York: Catholic Publication Society, 1869), 8.

24. "Spain," *Jewish Encyclopedia* 11:500; Roth, *Marranos*, 34; Waugh, *Europe*, 352-465; Kamen, *Spain: 1469-1714*, 38-44; Amador de los Rios, *Judíos* 2:191-220; López Martínez, *Judaizantes*, 187-252; Hope, *Torquemada*, 18-23, 197-200; "Inquisition," *Jewish Encyclopedia* 6:587-593; Beinart, "La inquisición española y la expulsión de los Judíos de Andalucía," *Jews and Conversos*, ed. Yoset Kaplan, 103-123; Adler, *Auto de Fé*, 53, 106-7; Garcia Boix, *Autos de Fé*, 1-6; and Beinart, *Records of the Trials* 1:xiii-xxxiv.

25. Valeriu Marcu, *Expulsion of the Jews from Spain*, trans. Moray Firth (London: Constable, 1935), 146-7.

26. "Provisión de los Reyes Católicos ordenando que los judíos salgan de sus reinos," *Documentos acerca de la Expulsión de los Judíos*, ed. Luís Suárez Fernández (Valladolid: CSIC, 1964), 391-95.

27. Baer, *Jews* 2:435.

28. William Thomas Walsh, *The Last Crusader: Isabella of Spain, 1541-1504* (Rockford, Ill.: Tan, 1987), 384; and Hare, *Queen*, 216.

29. Baer, *Jews* 2:315.

30. Carroll, *Isabel*, 124-5, 207; Nicolás González Ruíz, *Cisneros-Richelieu*, 2nd ed. (Barcelona: Cervantes, 1953), 58-60; D.Ch.J. Hefele, *Cardinal Jiménez de Cisneros* (Barcelona: Diario de Barcelona, 1869), 24-5, 125; H.G. Koenigsberger and Asa Briggs, *Early Modern Europe, 1500-1789* (London and New York: Longman, 1987), 73-4; Ximénez de Cisneros, *Catholic Encyclopedia* 14 (San Francisco: McGraw-Hill, 1967): 1062-3; Walter Starkie, *La España de Cisneros*, trans. Alberto Mestas (Barcelona: Juventud, 1943), 226-8; Juan de Vallejo, *Memorial de la Vida de Fray Francisco Jiménez de Cisneros*, ed. Antonio de la Torre y del Cerro (Madrid: Bailly-Bailliero, 1913), 5-6; Plunket, *Isabel*, 241-3; Baer, *Jews* 2:321-327; Longhurst, *Torquemada*, 47; Roth, *Marranos*, 49-51; Samuel Eliot Morison, *Admiral of the Ocean Sea* (Boston: Little Brown, 1942), 79-108; Jonathan D. Sarna, "Columbus and the Jews," *Commentary* 94 no. 5 (Nov. '92): 38-41; and Pike, *Enterprise & Adventure*, 3.

31. Walsh, *Isabel*, 369.

32. Abram, *Jewish Life*, 85, 306, 341; and Walsh, *Isabel*, 369-70.

33. Ibid., 371-2; B. Netanyahu, *Marranos of Spain* (New York: American Academy for Jewish Research, 1966), 235-45; Baer, *Jews* 2:488; Cutler and Cutler, *Jew*, 89-90, 98, 367; Carol Baroja, *Judíos*, 187-9; Marcu, *Expulsion*, 170; "Spain," *Jewish Encyclopedia* 11:501; Elnecave, *Hijos*, 99; Elkan Nathan Adler, *Auto de Fé and the Jew* (London: Oxford University Press, 1908), 55.

34. Salvador de Madariaga, *Spain: A Modern History* (New York: Praeger, 1958), 18.

35. Cutler and Cutler, *Jew*, 15-21, 81-120, 249-344; Kaplan, *Jews*, 84, 106-9; Baer, *Jews* 2:435-8; Plunket, *Isabel*, 267; Prescott, *Ferdinand* 1:352-5; and Roth, *Marranos*, 52.

36. St. Thomas Aquinas, *Summa Theologiae* (London and New York: Blackfriars, 1964), 91.

37. Carroll, *Isabel*, 210.

38. Baer, *Jews* 2:440-441.

39. Plunket, *Isabel*, 270.

40. Benjamin R. Gampel, *Last Jews on Iberian Soil* (Berkeley: University of California Press, 1989), 2, 10, 124-130; Elnecave, *Hijos*, 455-8; Roth, *Marranos*, 195-235; Allan Cowell, "Sephardim Celebrate 500 Good Years," *New York Times* (14 September '92), A4; and Marcu, *Expulsion*, 163.

41. Wayne Vucinich, *Ottoman Empire* (Huntington, NY: Krieger, 1979), 17; Lord Kinross, *Ottoman Centuries* (New York: Morrow Quill, 1977), 163; and George Castellan, *History of the Balkans,* Nicolas Brady, trans. (New York: Colombia University Press, 1992), 86, 88.

42. Dorothy Vaughan, *Europe and the Turk* (Liverpool: University Press, 1954), 87, 160-3; Robert Schwoebel, *Shadow of the Crescent* (New York: St. Martin's, 1967), 131; Gunther Rothenberg, *Austrian Military Border in Croatia, 1522-1747* (Urbana, IL: University Press, 1960, 1-2; L.S. Stavrianos, *Balkans Since 1453* (New York: Rinehart, 1958), 69, 156-7; and Norman Housley, *Later Crusades* (Oxford: University Press, 1992), 136-142, 294-300.

43. R.J. Rummel, *Death by Government* (New Brunswick, NY: Transaction Press, 1994), 1, 4 estimates 169,202,000 non-combatants have been victims of genocide in the twentieth century.

44. Hope, *Torquemada,* 211; Baer, *Jews* 2:436; Walsh, *Isabel,* 368-9; "Los Reyes Católicos Nombran a Abraham Senior Teseirero General de la Hermandad" 1488, Marzo 18, Valencia (*Documentos Sobre la Expulsion...,* 297-9; Elnecave, *Hijos,* 91, 314, 324; Roth, *Marranos,* 26; Faur, *Shadow,* 31, 44-5, 57; Americo Castro, *Teresa la Santa* (Madrid: Alfaguara, 1972), 245; Castro, *Structure,* 581-2; and Nicolas López Martínez, *Los judizantes castellanos y la Inquisición en el tiempo de Isabel la Católica* (Burgos: Semenario Metropolitano de Burgos, 1954), 143.

45. Morison, *Admiral,* 145, 158-9; Roth, *Marranos,* 273; and Marcu, *Expulsion,* 178.

46. Ibid., 162.

47. "500th Anniversary of Nebrija's Spanish Grammar," *España '92* 20, no. 225 (Madrid: Oct. '92): 13.

48. Jane S. Gerber, *Jews of Spain* (New York: Free Press-Macmillan, 1992), 261.

49. Ibid., 262-65; May, *Franco,* 72-6; "Revocación del Edicto de Expulsión," Elnecave, *Hijos,* 1008; Ibid., 251-4; "Spain," *Jewish Encyclopedia* 11:501; "Spain," *Encyclopedia Judaica* 15:244-5; Amador de los Rios, *Judíos* 2:3876-9; Adler, *Auto de Fé,* 9; Federico Ysart, *España y los Judíos en la Segunda Guerra Mundial* (Barcelona: Dopesa, 1973), 9-10, 43, 97; and Hiam Avni, Emanuel Shimoni, trans., *Spain: The Jews and Franco* (Philadelphia: Jewish Publication Society of America, 5747-1982), 103, 200-14.

50. "Sephard is no longer a sense of yearning," *España '92* 20, no. 221 (Madrid: May '92): 1.

Columbus as Biblical Exegete:
A Study of the *Libro de las profecías*

Hector Avalos

INTRODUCTION

Years before he sailed to the New World, Columbus had begun to link biblical prophecy with a voyage to the Orient. In particular, Columbus' notes to Aeneas Sylvius Piccolomini's (Pope Pius II) *Historia rerum ubique gestarum* reveal that he had already begun to think systematically about biblical prophecy around 1481. Eventually Columbus assembled an extensive collection of biblical prophecies and comments that is called the *Libro de las profecías*, a recent edition of which has been published by Delno West and August Kling.[1] The *Libro* is complete, except for the removal of some ten of its eighty-four folios.[2]

The extant form of the *Libro* was actually a transitional work insofar as Columbus intended to integrate or turn these prophecies into a poem (*para después tornarlas a rever y las poner en rima*).[3] The compilation of the major portion of the extant form of the *Libro* was completed between the third and fourth voyages, a time when Columbus' reputation and accomplishments were under siege.[4] More specifically, the composition is dated between September 13, 1501 and March 23, 1502 by West and Kling.[5] Only a very small part of the book was written in a hand identified by most scholars as that of Columbus. Father Gaspar Gorricio, a Carthusian monk, and Ferdinand, Columbus' son, are among those responsible for writing most of the book under Columbus' direction. Accordingly, one must be mindful that the *Libro* often reflects Columbus' use of scripture indirectly.

59

One of the most significant aspects of the research of the *Libro* is that until recently many major historians had minimized or refused altogether to acknowledge the importance of this work in the life of Columbus. Some would see Columbus' interest in prophecy as a sign of increasing senility or neurosis. For example, in 1984 Gianni Granzotto, a major Columbus biographer, attributed Columbus' compilation of the *Libro* to his advancing age, his infirmity, and his continual disappointments.[6] Other scholars have ignored it because the book reflects a part of Columbus that does not conform to the common image of him as a champion of modern cosmography.[7]

Columbus himself discusses the importance of biblical prophecy in his endeavors in an undispatched letter addressed to the King and Queen of Spain that introduces the *Libro:*

> Already I mentioned that for the execution of the voyage to the Indies I was not aided by reason, by mathematics, or by maps. It was simply the fulfillment of what Isaiah had said, and this is what I desire to write here.[8]

Although this passage provides a good argument for the importance of prophecy in Columbus' endeavors, its larger context, which we will examine below, also shows an opportunistic use of scripture in the promotion of his voyage.

Another important feature of the research of the *Libro* is that most of the study has been done, not by biblical scholars or students of the history of biblical exegesis, but by Columbian specialists and historians.[9] Fortunately, some of these historians, most notably Francisco Alvarez,[10] J.S. Cummins,[11] John V. Fleming,[12] Alain Milhou,[13] Pauline Watts,[14] and Delno West[15] have made very good observations on Columbus' use of the Bible.

This study aims to review from the viewpoint of biblical and exegetical scholarship the results of past research on the exegetical techniques and the eschatological framework that informed Columbus' view of himself and the New World. We shall add new observations on the variant readings of the Latin Bible found in the *Libro*, especially insofar as those variants have been used to assess Columbus' abilities as a scriptural scholar.

GENERAL EXEGETICAL PRINCIPLES

Columbus was conservative in his exegetical principles, following earlier medieval exegetical traditions without much deviation. In particular, Columbus draws repeatedly from the views of Pierre d'Ailly, Nicolas of Lyra, Joachim of Fiore, and Isidore of Seville.

Columbus' approach to prophetic interpretation was guided by the belief in different levels of "seeing." Citing the *Etymologies* of Isidore of Seville, the *Libro* discusses a tradition that holds that there are three types of prophetic vision. The first is one witnessed by the physical eyes of the body.[16] A second is called the "vision of the spirit" by which an "image is formed of things that can be sensed by the body."[17] A third "does not involve the physical senses or any part of the mind in which images of material things are formed, but as an intuition of the mind in which the truth appears and is understood."[18] As we shall see below, these distinctions were used by Columbus to counteract criticisms that his empirical data were insufficient to warrant a costly voyage.

Early in the *Libro* Columbus wished to establish the validity of the double meaning of prophecy (*duplex sensus litteralis*). In particular, he stresses the reversibility of tenses in the interpretation of prophecy:

It should be noted that in the Holy Scriptures the verbs in the past tense are sometimes used for the future, and so with the other tenses. . . .[19]

This was an ancient and pervasive exegetical principle that allowed Columbus to claim as prophecies many texts that, judging by the original grammar and context, otherwise refer to past events. Thus, in a section devoted to passages concerning "The Future" (*De futuro*), one finds many passages dealing with places (*e.g.*, Tarshish) involved in events that occurred in the days of the Old Testament (*e.g.*, 1 Kings 10:21-22; Jonah 1:3). However, those past events are viewed as prophecies that oblige Columbus to seek long lost biblical lands.

COLUMBUS AS A BIBLICAL SCHOLAR

If the *Libro* is any indication, Columbus and the other compilers were serious but not expert students of the Bible. For example, there is no solid evidence of knowledge of Hebrew in the *Libro*.[20] When some of the biblical passages in the *Libro* bear a closer proximity to the standard (Masoretic) Hebrew text than is reflected in the standard edition of the Vulgate, such proximity is usually a feature of the edition of the Latin Bible used by the compilers or their sources,[21] something that at most provides inconclusive evidence for Columbus' knowledge of Hebrew. Although Columbus himself quotes the famous Rabbi Samuel of Fez, the quotation is in Spanish.[22] Furthermore, in the book of Psalms, the *Libro* systematically prefers the Vulgate version based on the Greek text even when a version (the so-called *Hebraicum*) closer to the Masoretic Hebrew text was available.

More importantly, there is persuasive evidence that the Hebrew Bible or other Hebrew reference materials were not consulted. For example, in the section pertaining to Ophir, a place which Columbus assumes to be in India and identical with Tarshish and Kittim,[23] the *Libro* lists mostly passages in which the Hebrew word 'ôphîr is rendered in Latin as a transcription (*e.g.*, I Kings 9:28; 22:49). The *Libro* omits those passages where the Hebrew word is not transliterated, but instead rendered as "gold" (*e.g.*, Job 22:24), something that in itself is not very remarkable.

What is remarkable, however, is that the *Libro* omits the one passage, Job 28:16, where the Vulgate renders the Hebrew 'ôphîr precisely as "India." Had the compiler been aware of the underlying Hebrew word, we would expect him to regard this passage as the most important of all of the passages that might be used to argue that Ophir is India. Had the compiler used a good Hebrew concordance, he should have found all of the passages, about twelve in all, listing Ophir in Hebrew.[24] The example shows that Latin biblical aides were virtually the only ones consulted.

On the other hand, our study of the *Libro* reveals that the compilers were better scribes than West and Kling suggest. Regarding the scribal expertise reflected by the compilers of the *Libro*, West and Kling remark:

> The transcription of the Vulgate text is often faulty, with minor omissions and errors that seldom represent significant variations in meaning but that seem to reflect a copyist's lack of training and experience.[25]

and further, West and Kling infer:

> We would argue these faults as grounds for concluding that the

collaboration of Father Gaspar Gorricio (known otherwise to have been a skilled writer) was actually as limited as he claimed . . .[26]

However, closer inspection shows that the transcription of the Bible in the *Libro* was remarkably faithful and meticulous. West and Kling apparently assumed incorrectly that the modern Latin edition of the Vulgate[27] that they used for comparison with the passages in the *Libro* had remained immutable for centuries.

In our selective survey most of the readings that may be classified as errors or variations are actually attributable to the edition(s) of the Latin Vulgate used by the compilers of the *Libro*. For example, in Isaiah 18:2 West and Kling apparently regard as an "error"[28] on the part of the *Libro's* scribe (Ferdinand in this section) the addition of the following words that are not found in a modern standard edition of the Vulgate: *ad montem nominis Domini exercituum, montem Syon.* However, these words are found in the same place in Latin Bibles with Lyra's *Postilla litteralis*[29] published in 1492[30] and 1498.[31] We may summarize the readings in the different editions as follows:

Vulgate:[32]   [words not present]
Libro: ad montem nominis Domini exercituum, montem Syon
Lyra 1492:   ad montem nominis Domini exercituum montem Syon
Lyra 1498:   ad montem nominis domini exercitu(um) montem Sion

Thus, the transcription of the *Libro,* was quite faithful in this instance. There are other instances in which the *Libro* differs from the modern text of the Vulgate but agrees with the text of the Latin Bibles with Lyra's *Postilla litteralis* (1492 and/or 1498). Note the following examples all of that were transcribed by Gorricio:[33]

Isaiah 11:12   Isaiah 22:25
Vulgate: *levabit signum*   Vulgate: *die illo*
Libro: *levabit dominus signum*[34]   *Libro:*   *die illa*[35]
Lyra 1492: *levabit dominus signum*   Lyra 1492: *die illa*
                                                 Lyra 1498: *die illa*

Isaiah 25:7
Vulgate: *conligati*
Libro: *colligati*[36]
Lyra 1492:   *colligati*
Lyra 1498:   *colligati*

Isaiah 25:7
Vulgate: *super universas nationes*
Libro: *super omnes nationes*[37]
Lyra 1492:   *super o(mn)es*
Lyra 1498:   *super omnes nationes*

Isaiah 25:9
Vulgate: *dicet*
Libro: *dicent*[38]
Lyra 1492:   *dice(n)t*
Lyra 1498:   *dicent*

Isaiah 25:9
Vulgate: *eum exultabimus*
Libro: *et exultabimus*[39]
Lyra 1492:   *et exultabimus*
Lyra 1498:   *et exultabi(mus)*

Isaiah 27:13
Vulgate: *in terra Aegypti*
Libro: *de terra Egypti*[40]
Lyra 1492:   *d(e) terra Egypti*
Lyra 1498:   *de terra Egypti*

These examples are sufficient to show that the scribes of the *Libro* were probably copying from printed editions, and not paraphrasing or quoting from memory, as is sometimes assumed by some Columbian scholars. More importantly, West and Kling must either concede that the compilers of the *Libro* were better scribes than they thought, or that Gorricio (or a scribe deemed to be better than Columbus) made more of a contribution to the *Libro* than they suppose. Actually, the situation is complicated by the fact that some of the passages attributed to Gorricio have some of the most unique variants found in the *Libro* (*e.g.*, Isaiah 11:11, 25:6, and 55:1a discussed below).

Although the compiler of the *Libro* does not seem to change the wording of his biblical sources in order to bolster an argument, there is some evidence that passages contradicting a conclusion were omitted. For example, as previously mentioned, the *Libro* attempts to show that Kittim is a great source of gold located in the Orient. Although the *Libro* includes many passages that may suggest that Kittim is an oriental land, it omits 1 Maccabees 1:1 which suggests that the land of Kittim was Greece. Such an omission could not be due to lack of familiarity with the book of Maccabees because a number of citations drawn from I Maccabees (6:29, 14:5, and 15:1) shows that the compilers were well acquainted with that book.

On the other hand, determining the extent to which the biblical texts were copied faithfully or were changed for theological purposes requires a careful study of the editions used by the compilers. Unfortunately, the precise edition(s) of the Bible used by the compilers is still uncertain. The most recent editors of the *Libro* did not attempt to determine the precise edition(s), and D. West still has no knowledge of any attempts to determine the edition.[41] We can only provide some preliminary points of departure.

The most likely candidates are versions that are accompanied by the *Postilla litteralis* of Nicolas of Lyra simply because so many quotations in the *Libro* are accompanied by that commentary. Needless to say, the versions must be those published before 1505, the latest known date for the completion of the *Libro*, and after 1473, the earliest known date for the printing of Bibles with Lyra's *Postilla litteralis*.[42]

Our brief comparison shows that the *Libro's* text of Lyra's commentary on Daniel 8,[43] transcribed by an unidentified hand, is more often in agreement with the edition of 1498 than with the one of 1492. For example:

Libro:	*aliquando est duplex sensus litteralis*
Lyra 1492:	*aliquando est duplex sententia litteralis*
Lyra 1498:	*aliquando est duplex sensus litteralis*

Libro:	*ideo quando in veteri testamento*
Lyra 1492:	*et ideo quando in veteri testamento*
Lyra 1498:	*ideo quando in veteri testamento*

Libro:	*unus minus principalis*
Lyra 1492:	*un(us) principalis*
Lyra 1498:	*unus minus principalis*

Although our brief survey of variants in Isaiah has shown a relationship between the readings in the *Libro* and the Latin Bibles of 1492 and 1498, those editions were probably not the ones used by the compilers of the *Libro*. The reason is that there are readings in the *Libro* that are not found in either of those editions. The following are a few examples (scribe in parenthesis):

Isaiah 11:11 (Gorricio)

Libro: Ennam[44]

Vulgate: Aelam

Lyra 1492: Elam

Lyra 1498: elam

Isaiah 24:16 (Ferdinand)

Libro: vidimus[45]

Vulgate: audivimus

Lyra 1492: audivimus

Lyra 1498: audivimus

Isaiah 25:6 (Gorricio)

Libro: exercitum in monte hoc[46]

Vulgate: exercituum omnibus populis in monte hoc

Lyra 1492: exercituum o(mni)b(us) populi(s) i(n) mo(n)te hoc

Lyra 1498: exercituu(m) o(mni)b(us) populi(s) i(n) mo(n)te h(oc)

Isaiah 55:1a (Gorricio)

Libro: edite[47]

Vulgate: emite

Lyra 1492: emite

Lyra 1498: emite

As in the case of the other readings, it would be premature to declare the sometimes unexpected readings (e.g., Ennam instead of Elam) in the *Libro* as scribal "errors" until a more systematic comparison with other Latin Bibles from the period is undertaken. Such a systematic comparison is one of the most important unfinished tasks in the study of the *Libro*.

THE *LIBRO* AS AN ARGUMENT FOR THE SPONSORSHIP OF COLUMBUS' VOYAGES

The *Libro* appears to be the product of a complex person who is both a sincere believer and an astute promoter of his own interests. In particular, Columbus' letter to the monarchs of Spain reveals a very astute use of scripture to promote his first voyage. For example, at the time that he proposed his voyage, Columbus' scientific data and argumentation were criticized widely. A commission appointed by the monarchs to study Columbus' proposals in the late 1480s complained that he had very little data that could be verified empirically or mathematically. Columbus himself spoke of the derisive treatment which he received from the most learned men of the court.

> I spent seven years here in your royal court discussing this subject with the leading persons in all the learned arts, and

their conclusion was that all was in vain. . . . All those who know me and who see this book will privately or even publicly reproach me by various kinds of criticism: that I am unlearned in literature, a laymen, a mariner, a common worldly man, etc. I respond to this in the words of Matthew (11:25) "O Lord . . . because thou has hid these things from the wise and prudent and revealed them to little ones."[48]

He interpreted Matthew 11:25 to mean that he was one of these "little ones," a reference to his then obscure reputation and status.[49] Thus, this passage is a prime example of how Columbus saw the Bible as the refuge and defender of a man who did not possess the data considered decisive by the monarchs' advisors. Indeed, he later argues in the same letter that the best proof of his mission is not found in scientific data, but in the prophecies of scripture that he has earnestly studied.

In the absence of an empirically based cosmography or verifiable information concerning a westward route to the Indies, Columbus chose an authority that his listeners could not dismiss as easily. Thus, Columbus may be categorized as an opportunist in using biblical prophecies to compensate repeatedly for the lack of scientific data requested by many of the monarch's advisors. Columbus' strategy was to convince the monarchs that biblical cosmography was equal or better than any cosmography derived from extra-biblical methods. For Columbus, biblical data were, if interpreted properly, empirical and verifiable data.

Columbus' efforts to counteract unfavorable non-biblical measurements of the westward distance to the Orient also were undoubtedly behind his strenuous support for the divine origin and prophetic value of 2 Esdras, a deutero-canonical work. In his notes to Piccolomini's *Historia rerum ubique gestarum* Columbus explicitly mounts a defense of the prophetic, albeit non-canonical, authenticity of 2 Esdras.[50] He also enlists the help of, among other authorities, St. Ambrose, St. Augustine, and Peter Comester.[51]

It was to Columbus' advantage to provide all the available evidence to show that the westward distance between Spain and the Orient was small. 2 Esdras 6:42 stated that only one seventh of the planet was made of water, and the rest was inhabitable land. Since 2 Esdras 6:42 suggested that the total amount of water on the planet was quite small, Columbus could claim scriptural support for the existence a small body of water between Spain and the Orient.[52]

Another main goal of Columbus' work was to show that biblical prophecies obliged him and the Spanish monarchs to, among other things, sponsor a voyage to the Indies. This goal is most evident in Columbus' relatively small set of explicit and implicit criteria for his selection of biblical passages. He states his explicit criteria as follows:

> Here begins the book, [or handbook, of s]ources, statements opinions, and p[rophecies on] the subject of the recovery of God's holy city and Mount Zion, and on the discovery and evangelization of the island of the Indies and of all other peoples and nations.[53]

Since "islands" apparently were considered a reference to the farthest lands remaining to be evangelized, he devotes a section to "things written about islands of the sea in the Holy Scriptures" (*Hec de insulis maris scripta sunt in sacra Scriptura*).[54] The neat sequence of passages indicates that the compilers were aided by a concordance in this section. Although nearly thirty-six passages mentioning the word "island(s)" may be found in the Bible, the *Libro* bears twenty-six for this section.[55]

Not surprisingly, the *Libro* includes passages that speak about God's future dealings with the islands. For example: Isaiah 51:5: "The islands shall look for me and shall patiently wait for my arm."[56] As in other sections of the *Libro* that speak of distant countries, passages that may be interpreted as commands to preach to these islands are also invariably present. For example, Jeremiah 31:10: "Hear the word of the Lord, O ye nations, and declare it in the islands that are afar off."[57]

If the reader might not be convinced that these "far lands" refer to the Orient, Columbus attempts to corroborate the identification by adding notes. For example, Jeremiah 16:19 states: "To thee shall the nations come from the ends of the earth and say: 'Surely our fathers have worshipped mendacious idols.'" Columbus comments: "India is in the farthest lands in the east. . . . In India, they venerate and raise up idols."[58]

As expected, passages that mentioned water also were well represented. Although most explorers knew or believed that India and other important places in the Far East were reachable by land, the numerous passages involving the sea apparently were meant to show that the Bible favored maritime, and not overland, expeditions to the Far East. For Columbus, passages such as 1 Kings 10:21-22 clearly showed that maritime journeys to the Orient (= Tarshish for

Columbus) were preferred by the wisest king in ancient Israel, Solomon:

> For the king's navy, once every three years, went with the navy of Hiram by sea to Tharsis; and brought from thence gold, and silver . . .[59]

Although there is no reason to doubt his belief in the prophecies he collects, Columbus weaves them into the argument that his explorations should be sponsored as soon as possible. He explicitly says that the scriptures urge him to "press forward with haste, without hesitating for even a moment."[60]

Why the hurry? The answer is found in the previously mentioned undispatched letter to the King and Queen of Spain. Here Columbus adduces the calculations of King Alfonso "The Wise" (1221-1284) to argue that only 150 years are left until the completion of 7,000 years of human history. At the completion of the 7,000 years Christ was to return to earth to inaugurate the blissful millennium that all Christians awaited. Columbus adds concerning these calculations: "This tells me that the Gospel must now be proclaimed to so many lands in a very short time."[61] In short, the evangelization of non-Christian lands was a prerequisite for the establishment of the Millennium, and the Orient was viewed as one of the last areas that remained to be evangelized.

As mentioned above Columbus explicitly stated that the recapture of Zion was one of the main criteria for his selection of passages. Thus, Psalm 51:18 (Lat. 50:20): "Deal favorably, O Lord, in thy good will with Sion; that the walls of Jerusalem may be built up."[62] He states: "Jerusalem and Mount Zion shall be built by the hand of Christians."[63]

The rebuilding of Zion is viewed by Columbus within an apocalyptic framework. Indeed, Columbus knew of the traditions that heralded King Ferdinand as the conqueror of Jerusalem. Prophecies that identified Ferdinand (alone or jointly with Isabella) as the monarch who would recapture Jerusalem were known from as early as 1473, and were based on an earlier tradition that affirmed the messianic character of Spanish kings.[64]

Concerning the rebuilder of the Temple, Columbus states: "The abbot Joachim [of Fiore] said that he would come from Spain."[65] Not surprisingly, he often reinterpreted the addressee in the passages that speak of the rebuilding of Zion and the Temple. For example, in Psalm 20:2 (Lat. 19:3; "May he send thee help from the sanctuary; and defend

thee out of Sion"),[66] Columbus assumed that the addressee was the
Spanish monarchs or some other Christian crusader. Such prophecies
would be useful in flattering and coaxing the monarchs into action. On
the other hand, Columbus' collection of prophecies, filled with so
many imperatives, added a sense of obligation and urgency to his pleas.
Again, Columbus' efforts to persuade the monarchs to rebuild
Jerusalem is linked to the belief that the rebuilding of the temple was
a prerequisite for the establishment of the Millennium.

The *Libro* selected a variety of passages that supposedly showed that
the Indies were the gold-laden lands called Ophir, Tarshish, and Kittim
in the Bible. Thus, he includes Psalm 72:10 (Lat. 71:10), a passage that
promises monetary rewards: "The kings of Tharsis and the islands shall
offer presents."[67] Again, Columbus apparently uses the Bible to entice
the king into a profitable enterprise. At the same time Columbus
wished to persuade the monarchs to use at least part of the gold for the
recapture of Jerusalem. In fact, in his journal entry of December 26,
1492, Columbus states:

> I complained to your Highnesses that all of the profit from my
> enterprise should be spent in the conquest of Jerusalem,
> whereat your Highnesses smiled and said that it pleased
> them.[68]

If he really believed this, then Columbus saw his voyage, in large part,
as an effort to finance the capture of Jerusalem.[69] The fact that
Columbus was serious about using New World gold to finance the
recapture of Jerusalem is evident in his will and testament dated 22
February, 1498.[70] That will includes a clause that prescribes that a
portion of the annual income from his estate be deposited in the Bank
of Saint George (of Genoa) as a revolving fund destined for financing
a crusade for the liberation of the Holy Sepulchre in Jerusalem.[71]

BIBLICAL EXEGESIS AND NEW WORLD POLICY

Aside from searching for biblical support to promote his voyage,
Columbus' *Libro* also reveals the biblical basis for policies pursued in
the New World by Spain.[72] Columbus' policy to enslave and
evangelize began to be executed, by his own words, as soon as he met
the natives. Columbus' journal entry (dated October 11, 1492) about his
first encounter with native peoples says:

They should make good slaves .... I believe that they will easily become Christians.[73]

The policies of Columbus and his successors were rooted in the ideas expressed in many biblical passages selected in the *Libro*. For example, Psalm 9:20 (and 10:16; Lat. 9:21, 37), in part, states:

Appoint O Lord, a lawgiver over them: that the Gentiles may know themselves to be but men ... ye Gentiles shall perish from his land.[74]

Columbus clearly believed that the native people he saw were the Gentiles of whom this and other passages spoke.

Further evidence that such passages did influence his plans for the treatment of the native cultures of the New World is found in Columbus' own marginal comments on Augustine's *On the Divination of Demons* that assesses Zephaniah 2:11 as follows:

These quotations, and others like them taken from the prophets, demonstrate sufficiently ... that one day the God of Israel, whom we recognize as the only true God, will be worshipped not merely by a single nation called the people of Israel, but among all the Gentile nations, and that he will destroy all the false gods from their temples and from the heart of their Gentile worshippers.[75]

For Columbus, scriptures such as Zephaniah 2:11 meant that the process of converting non-Christians had to involve the systematic and violent destruction of non-Christian religions.[76] In addition, for Columbus and other Europeans[77] who followed him, such passages provided divine authorization for the imposition of European laws upon the conquered territories, and for the systematic destruction of the native cultures that resisted Christianization.

Ironically, Columbus also saw the New World as the place where one could find the biblical paradise. One of the most detailed discussions of this view is found not in the *Libro* but, among other places, in a letter describing the Gulf of Paria (between Venezuela and Trinidad) that he visited on the third voyage (1498). For Columbus, the area's powerful rivers and their extraordinarily fresh waters were empirical evidence that he was near "the terrestrial paradise, where no one can enter without divine permission."[78]

Such an idea produces a most paradoxical picture of the New World. On the one hand, it is a sinful land in need of redemption by Christians. On the other, it is the land that contains the sinless paradise which is unapproachable by Christians, except with special permission.

It is remarkable that such speculations about paradise are not very dominant in the *Libro*. Genesis 2:8-3:24, which is the biblical *locus classicus* on the geography of Eden, is not cited in the *Libro*. Thus, it appears that his discovery of "paradise" either had no eschatological significance for Columbus, or that he had moved toward seeing the New World as an absolutely godless land, all of which could be conquered and treaded upon by Christians.

We have mentioned Columbus' collection of biblical passages which he believed supported claims that large gold reserves were to be found in the New World. Columbus and the Crown appear to have had different views and policies concerning the gold found in the New World. Columbus argued that the gold was to be used to finance the recapture of Jerusalem, while the monarchs were apparently more interested in using the gold to, among other things, repay debts incurred by wars earlier in their reigns.

THE *LIBRO* AS AN INCOMPLETE EPIC

The list of passages assembled by Columbus may be viewed as a data bank of scriptural support for his mission. His collection addresses known and possible objections to, among other things, Columbus' ideas concerning the profitability of the mission, the westward distance to the Orient, and the royal obligation to finance the conquest of Jerusalem.

But since Columbus knew that he had been vindicated when he began to write the extant form of the *Libro* in 1501-02, the purpose of this work must be viewed differently after his initial voyages. As mentioned above, Columbus intended to integrate the prophecies into a poem. This poem, however, was to be nothing less than an epic with Columbus as the hero.

Cogent testimony for this particular intention may be found in his translation into Spanish of Seneca's *Tragedy of Medea*.[79] The original Latin of Seneca's work says (in English translation):

The time will come
in a number of years, when Oceanus

will unfasten the bounds, and a huge
Land will stretch out, and Typhis the
pilot will discover new worlds, so
The remotest land will no longer be Thule.[80]

However, Columbus' Spanish translation (in English) reads:

In the latter years of the world will come certain times in
which the Ocean sea will relax the bonds of things, and a great
land will open up, *and new mariner like the one who was the
guide of Jason*, whose name was Typhis, will discover a new world,
and then will the island of Thule no longer be the farthest land.[81]

By adding "and a new mariner like the one who was the guide of
Jason" to Seneca's poem, Columbus' inserts himself in that prophecy.
This insertion shows that he saw himself as a great voyager and the
equal or better than those mentioned in classical literature. Columbus'
poem, in effect, would be a sort of new *Odyssey*.

Viewed in this manner, the biblical passages were no longer simply
a list of evidences for the correctness of biblical cosmography, but they
were also God's own testimonials to Columbus' wisdom and glory.
Each biblical passage collected in the *Libro* becomes a paean to
Columbus' importance in human history.

Although still in a preliminary stage, the structure of the *Libro* may
have been designed to show Columbus' own glorious rise. As
previously mentioned, near the beginning of the *Libro* there is the letter
addressed to Ferdinand and Isabella that details how the royal court
humiliated Columbus. At this stage he acknowledges that he is one of
the "little ones" mentioned by Matthew 11:25. The body of the *Libro*
consists of the prophecies that, among other things, are meant to refute
the opinion of the wise men of the royal court. Near the end of the
Libro is his translation of Seneca's poem in which he identifies himself,
not as "a little one," but as the hero of an epic. While more prophecies
follow Seneca's poem, one may speculate on whether the structure of
the *Libro* was intended to highlight the fact that, although he began his
career as "a little one," Columbus now was ending his life as one of
history's greatest men. His exploits are prophesied in biblical and
classical literature.

CONCLUSION

The *Libro* is a remarkable record of Columbus' view of himself and the New World. The new edition of the *Libro* hopefully will finally lay to rest any thought that Columbus' interest in prophecy was a product of senility or personal idiosyncrasies. Columbus had a longstanding interest in prophecy, and he was in the mainstream of most eschatological speculations of the Middle Ages.[82] Far from being the champion of modern cosmography, the *Libro* shows that Columbus championed Medieval and bibliocentric cosmographies to his dying day.

The function of the prophecies collected by Columbus is as complex as the man himself, and probably evolved in phases. Prior to his first voyage, Columbus' collection of biblical prophecies was probably meant to serve as a compendium for his propaganda. This, of course, does not imply that he did not believe in those prophecies or in his own propaganda. In any event, during this stage, it is improbable that he was thinking about using these scriptures in an epic poem about his future discoveries.

However, since Columbus began to make the most substantive compilations long after he had been vindicated by the triumph of 1492, the prophecies in the *Libro* cannot be viewed simply as a compendium of biblical passages that he could use to justify his enterprise. Such a justification was no longer needed after 1492. After the latter date, the collection of prophecies by Columbus are best viewed as an effort to create a self-congratulatory epic that would be the equal or better of the *Iliad* and the *Odyssey*.

But Columbus saw his mission as much more than a heroic epic about maritime expeditions. In order to understand the true magnitude of his self-image, one must turn to his eschatological framework. In his now classic *The Pursuit of the Millennium*, Norman Cohn[83] attempted to show that eschatological speculation, far from being on the fringe of history, was one of its major driving forces. The *Libro* shows the important role of eschatology in Columbus' enterprise. If we follow his own reasoning, Columbus believed that no more than 150 years were left until the Second Coming of Jesus. In order to expedite the Second Coming, Columbus believed that two tasks had to be completed: 1) the conversion of non-Christian peoples, and 2) the conquest of Jerusalem and the rebuilding of the Temple. His enterprise intended to reach non-Christians as quickly as possible by sailing westward. His search for gold in these lands was motivated, not so much by personal greed, but by his plan to find sufficient gold to finance the conquest of

Jerusalem. In short, Columbus saw himself as no less than the man who would pave the way for the Second Coming of Jesus. Ironically, Columbus' beliefs about the impending end of the world resulted in the discovery of a new one.

NOTES

1. Delno West and August Kling, *The Libro de las profecías of Christopher Columbus* (Gainesville: U. of Florida, 1991). Henceforth, all citations discussed here will be from their edition, and abbreviated as *Libro*. English translations, unless otherwise noted, are those of West and Kling.

2. For a detailed discussion about the physical state of the book and the debates surrounding motives for the removal of some of the pages, see West and Kling, *Libro*, 82-83.

3. On the expression of Columbus' intentions in a letter to Father Gorricio, see West and Kling, *Libro*, 80. Spanish citations in the *Libro* may deviate from standard Spanish orthography.

4. Administrative fiascos in the New World, among other events, culminated in his return to Spain in fetters at the end of the third voyage. For further details, see West and Kling, *Libro*, 8-9.

5. West and Kling, *Libro*, 80. The editors (page 86) also note that Columbus may have been enlarging the book as late as 1505.

6. Gianni Granzotto, *Cristoforo Colombo* (Milan: Arnoldo Mondadori, 1984), 292: *per l'età che avanzava, la infermità delle membra, le delusioni dello spiritu.* For a fundamental biography with a relatively more balanced view of the role of Columbus' eschatology, see Antonio Ballesteros Beretta, *Cristobal Colon y el Descubrimiento de America*, 2 vols. (Barcelona y Buenos Aires: Salvat, 1945).

7. See further, Delno West, "Wallowing in a Theological Stupor or a Steadfast and Consuming Faith: Scholarly Encounters with Columbus' *Libro de las Profecias,*" in Donald T. Gerace, ed., *Proceedings First San Salvador Conference: Columbus and His World* (San Salvador Island, Bahamas, 1987), 45-56.

8. *Libro*, 110: *Ye dise que para la hesecución de la ynpresa de las Yndias no me aprovechó rasón ni matemática, ni mapamundos; llenamente se cunplió lo que diso Ysaýas. Y esto es lo que deseo de escrevir aquí.*

9. John V. Fleming, "Christopher Columbus as a Scriptural Exegete," *Lutheran Quarterly* 5, no. 2 (1991): 197 says: "There is, so far as I know, no study of his exegesis. I hope this may serve as a beginning." Despite the wide scope implied in the title of his study, Fleming focuses mainly on the significance of the number 22 in some of Columbus' discussion of the number of books in the Bible.

10. Francisco Alvarez, "Cristóbal Colón y el estudio de la Sagrada Escritura," *Archivo Hispalense* 17 (1952): 129-140.

11. J.S. Cummins, "Christopher Columbus: Crusader, Visionary, and *Servus dei*," in *Medieval Hispanic Studies Presented to Rita Hamilton*, ed. A.D. Deyermond (London, 1976), 45-55.

12. John V. Fleming, "Christopher Columbus as a Scriptural Exegete," *Lutheran Quarterly* 5 (2, 1991): 187-198.

13. Alain Milhou, *Colón y su mentalidad mesiánica en el ambiente franciscanista español* (Museo de Colón: Valladolid, 1983).

14. Pauline Watts, "Prophecy and Discovery: On the Spiritual Origins of Christopher Columbus' 'Enterprise of the Indies,'" *American Historical Review* 90 (1, 1985): 102.

15. West, "Wallowing in a Theological Stupor," 45-56.

16. *Libro,* 134: *Unum secundum oculos corporis. . . .*

17. *Libro,* 134: *Alterum secundum spiritum, quo imaginamur ea que per corpus sentimus. . . .*

18. *Libro,* 136: *Tertium autem genus visionis est quod neque corporeis sensibus, neque ulla parte anime qua corporalium rerum imagines capiuntur, sed per intuitum mentis quo intellecta conspicitur veritas.*

19. *Libro,* 102: *Notandum quod in Sacra Scriptura aliquando ponitur tempus pro tempore, sicut preteritum pro futuro.*

20. The determination of knowledge of Hebrew by Columbus is also of interest to those scholars who have followed the controversial thesis, most forcefully expounded by Salvador de Madariaga in *Christopher Columbus* (London: Hollis and Carter, 1949), especially 408-415, that Columbus was a converted Jew. See further, Ruth G. Durlach-Wolper, "The Identity of Christopher Columbus," in Gerace, *Proceedings First San Salvador Conference: Columbus and His World*, 13-32; Sarah Leibovici, *Christophe Colomb juif (Paris, 1986)*; M. Pollak, "The Ethnic Background of Columbus: Inference from a Genoese-Jewish Source, 1553-1557," *Revista de Historia de America* 80 (1975): 147-64; Juan Gil, "Colón y la Casa Santa," *Historiografía y Bibliografía Americanistas* 21 (1977): 125-35; Simon Wiesenthal, *Sails of Hope: The Secret Mission of Christopher Columbus*, trans. R. and C. Winston (New York: Macmillan, 1973).

21. For example, in Exodus 23:24, the Vulgate (citing the edition of Weber) reads: *et confringes statuas eorum.* The *Libro,* 148 reads: *et confringendo confringes simulacra eorum.* In contrast to the translation of the Vulgate, the words *confringendo confringes* in the *Libro* follow the Masoretic text which uses here a familiar Hebrew construction consisting of the infinitive absolute plus verb of the same root (*harēs tĕharsēm*). The source of the biblical quotation in the *Libro,* however, is actually Augustine's *Harmony of the Gospels,* Book 1, Chapter 29.

22. It is difficult to attribute to Columbus a knowledge of Hebrew on the basis of his quotation of Rabbi Samuel of Fez (Morrocco) who lived in the eleventh century. The latter's works were widely read and circulated in Latin, Catalan and Castillian during Columbus' lifetime. See further Milhou, *Colón y su mentalidad mesianica*, 157-159.

23. The *Libro* (240) depends principally on Nicolas of Lyra for this identification. For other traditions regarding Ophir in the time of Columbus, see Juan Gil, *Mitos y Utopias del Descubrimiento* (Madrid: Alianza Editorial, 1989), 52-56.

24. Solomon Mandelkern, (*Veteris Testamenti concordantiae hebraicae atque chaldaicae* (Lipsiae, 1896) lists twelve passages at most.

25. *Libro*, 96.

26. Ibid.

27. West and Kling, *Libro*, 96 state: "The Vulgate *textus receptus* has served as the basis for most of the quotations from the Bible found in the *Libro de las profecías*." West and Kling do not specify which edition of the Vulgate they regard as a representative of the *textus receptus*, but they are apparently relying on the Sixto-Clementine edition via the Douay Version. See further, Hector Ignacio Avalos, "The Biblical Sources of Columbus' *Libro de las Profecías*," *Traditio* 49 (1994): 331-335.

28. West and Kling, *Libro*, 219, do not translate this portion of the Latin into English, thus apparently indicating that it is not part of the original biblical text.

29. For a list of printed editions of Lyra's commentary, see Edward A. Gosselin, "A Listing of the Printed Editions of Nicolaus of Lyra," *Traditio* 26 (1970): 399-426.

30. The edition of 1492 (henceforth cited as Lyra 1492), which reproduces the edition of Johan (Reinhard) Grüningen, is based on an exemplar at the Stiftsbibliothek of Aschaffenburg, and it is catalogued by the U. of North Carolina-Chapel Hill as *Nicolaus de Lyra, Postilla super totam bibliam* (Strassburg, 1492 [repr. Frankfurt: Minerva, 1971]). This is presumably the same edition catalogued as #38 by Gosselin, "Listing," 409.

31. This edition (cited henceforth as Lyra 1498) is cited as #48 by Gosselin, "Listing," 410. We have used a copy at the University of North Carolina at Chapel Hill which is catalogued in part as: *Biblia Latina . . . cum postillas ac moralitatibus Nicolai d Lyra . . .* (Basel: Johann Froben and Joahnn Petri, 1 December, 1498).

32. Vulgate (in all comparisons with the *Libro*, "Vulgate" refers to the edition of Weber), *Biblia sacra iuxta Vulgatam versionem*, 3rd ed. (Stuttgart: Deutsche Bibelgesellschaft, 1983).

33. The identification of the scribes is that of West and Kling *Libro*, 81-83. We use parentheses to represent letters that are subsumed in ligatures or abbreviations in the Latin texts.

34. *Libro*, 164.

35. *Libro,* 168.

36. *Libro,* 164.

37. Ibid.

38. Ibid.

39. Ibid.

40. *Libro,* 166.

41. Delno West, personal communication, April 2, 1992.

42. Dates as reflected in Gosselin, "Listing," 408-411.

43. *Libro,* 102-104.

44. *Libro,* 164.

45. *Libro,* 168.

46. Ibid.

47. Ibid.

48. *Libro,* 106-07: *Siete años pasé aqui en su real corte, disputando el caso con tantas personas de tanta abtoridad y sabios en todas artes, y en fin concluyeron que todo hera vano . . . todos los otros que me consosçen, y á quien esta escritura fuere amostrada, que en secreto ó públicamente me reprehenderán de reprehensión de diversas maneras: de non doto en letras, de lego marinero, de honbre mundanal &c. Respondo aquello, que dixo san Mateus "O Señor, que quisistes tener secreto tantas cosas á los sabios y rebelástelas á los ynoçentes!"*

49. The Franciscans, with whom Columbus had an intimate association, also used this expression to refer to themselves. See further Milhou, *Colón y su mentalidad mesiánica,* 92-95.

50. 2 Esdras, known also as IV Ezra, is an apocalyptic work that has received new attention. See for example, Michael E. Stone, *Fourth Ezra* (Minneapolis: Fortress, 1990).

51. Martín F. de Navarrete, *Viages de Colón* (Mexico City: Porrua, 1825), 270.

52. On more specific measurements of the westward distance to the Orient used by Columbus, see Georges A. Charlier, "The Value of the Mile used by Columbus," in Gerace, *Proceedings First San Salvador Conference: Columbus and His World,* 115-120.

53. *Libro,* 100: *Incipit liber s[ive manipulus de au]ctoritatibus, dictis, ac sententiis et p[rophetiis circa] materiam recuperande sancta civitatis, et monti Dei Syon, ac inventionis & conversionis insularum Indie et omnium gentium nationum.* The citations in the *Libro* do not always derive from the biblical books one usually associates with eschatology. For example, Daniel and Revelation played relatively minor parts in the *Libro,* with only a total of about eight citations. In contrast, the Books of Chronicles were cited about thirty-six times, probably because of the number of references to maritime lands and expeditions. Columbus has indicated his fondness of Isaiah (about fifty-five citations), but most citations come from the Psalms (over 120 citations). Columbus also used non-biblical sources as prophecies, and these included Seneca.

54. *Libro*, 248.

55. According to West and Kling, *Libro*, 24, there is an extant concordance known to have been owned by Columbus, namely *Concordantiae Bibliae Cardinalis S.P.*, an anonymous and undated work (probably fifteenth-century).

56. *Libro*, 250: *Me insule ex[s]pectabunt, et brachium meum sustinenbunt.*

57. *Libro*, 252: *Audite verbum Domine, gentes, et annuntiate in insulis que procul sunt.*

58. *Libro*, 146: *India est in extremo :erre, in oriente. . . . Iam Indi veniunt et evertunt ydola.*

59. *Libro*, 240: *quia classis regis per mare cum classe Hyram semel per tres annos ibat in Tharsis; deferens inde aurum, et argentum. . . .*

60. *Libro*, 104: *sin çesar un momento, me abiban con gran prisa.*

61. *Libro*, 110: *el predicar del Evangelio en tantas tierras de tan poco tiempo acá me lo dice.*

62. *Libro*, 116: *Benigne fac in bona voluntate tua Syon et edificentur muri Ierusalem. . . .*

63. de Navarrete, *Viages de Colón*, 299: *Hierusalem y el monte Sion ha de ser reedificado por mano de cristianos.*

64. For a list of these prophecies, see Milhou, *Colón y su mentalidad mesiánica*, 389-400.

65. de Navarrete, *Viages de Colón*, 299: *El abad Joaquín dijo que éste había de salir de España.* There is no known writing of Joachim which contains such a tradition.

66. *Libro*, 114: *Mittat tibi auxilium de sancto et de Syon tueatur te.*

67. *Libro*, 248: *Reges Tharsis, et insule, munera offerent.*

68. Alvar, *Diario 2*: 180: *. . . que así (dize él) protesté á Vuestras Altezas que toda la ganançia d' esta mj empresa se gastase en la conquista de Hierusalém, y Vuestras Altezas se rieron y dixeron que les plazía.*

69. See further, Juan Gil, "Colón y la Casa Santa," *Historiografía y Bibliografía Americanistas* 21 (1977): 125-35.

70. Cesare de Lollis, *Raccolta di documente e Studi Pubblicazione a cura della Regia Commissione Colombianna nel quarto centenario dalla scoperta dell'America*, Part 1 (Rome: 1892-94), 310.

71. Leonard I. Sweet, "Christopher Columbus and the Millennial Vision of the New World," *Catholic Historical Review* 72, no. 3 (1986): 382 n. 47, argues against scholars *e.g.*, John Leddy Phelan, *The Millennial Kingdom of the Franciscans in the New World*, 2nd. ed. (Berkeley, Calif., 1970), 19, who believe that Columbus' last testament (August 25, 1505) omitted this provision.

72. For treatments of the influence of millennialism on New World policies, see Phelan, *The Millennial Kingdom of the Franciscans in the New World;* Sweet, "Christopher Columbus," 369-382, 715-16; and Djelal Kadir, *Columbus and the Ends of the Earth: Europe's Prophetic Rhetoric as Conquering Ideology* (Berkeley: U. of California Press, 1992).

73. Quotation from the critical edition of Manuel Alvar, *Diario del Descubrimiento*, 2 vols., 2 (Gran Canaria: Cabildo Insular de Gran Canaria, 1976): 53: *deben ser buenos servidores . . . creo que ligeramente se harían cristianos.* The word "servidor" could mean servant in the sense of "servant of Christ," however, it is clear from the context that he meant the word in the sense of a physical laborer as well.

74. *Libro*, 112: *Constitue, Domine, legislatorem super eos . . . peribitis gentes de terra illius.*

75. *Libro*, 154, 156: *Hiis atque huiusmodi propheticis documentis predictum ostenditur . . . futurum fuisse ut Deum Israel, quem unum Deum verum intelligunt, non in una ipsa gente que a[p]pellata est Israel, sed in omnibus gentibus coleretur, et omnes falsos deos gentium et a templis eorum et a cordibus cultorum suorum demoliretur.* Columbus' marginal notes read: *"attende diligenter"* ["Heed well"].

76. Zephaniah 2:11 reads in part (as quoted in the *Libro*, 154): *Deus adversus eos, et exterminabit omnes deos gentium terre* [The Lord shall prevail against them, and he shall exterminate all the gods of the nations of the earth].

77. For example, Jeronimo de Mendieta, *Historia Eclesiastica Indiana*, ed. F. Solano y Perez-Lila, 1 (Madrid: Biblioteca de Autores Españoles 260, 1973): 107-115, a vigorous apologist of Spanish policies in the New World, argues specifically that Cortez, the conqueror of Mexico, should be viewed as another Moses, the lawgiver and liberator.

78. de Navarrete, *Viages de Colón*, 269: *creo que alli est el paraiso terrenal adonde no puede llegar nadie, salvo por voluntad divina.*

79. From the Chorus, *audax nimium* in Book 7.

80. As recorded in the *Libro*, 224: *Venient annis/secula seris, quibus Oceanus/vincula rerum laxet, & ingens/pateat te[l]us Tiphisque novos/ detegat orbes, nec sit terris/ ultima Tille.* I have used slashes to indicate new lines in the *Libro's* arrangement of the poem.

81. *Libro*, 226: *Vernán los tardos años del mundo ciertos tiempos en los quales el mar Ocçéano afloxerá los atamentos de las cosas, y se abrirá una grande tierra, y um nuebo marinero como aquél que fué guya de Jasón que obe nombre Tiphi, descobrirá nuebo mundo, y entonçes no será la ysla Tille la postrera de las tierras.*

82. For a summary of such speculations, see Richard K. Emmerson, *The Antichrist in the Middle Ages* (Seattle: U. of Washington Press, 1981).

83. Norman Cohn, *The Pursuit of the Millennium* (New York: Oxford, 1957). See also, Delno C. West, "Christopher Columbus, Lost Biblical Sites, and the Last Crusade," *The Catholic Historical Review* 78 (October, 1992): 519-541.

The Mythical Jewish Columbus
and the History of America's Jews

Jonathan D. Sarna

All across the United States, Wednesday October 12, 1892, the 400th anniversary of Christopher Columbus' landing in the New World was celebrated with great fanfare. New York, where the most memorable commemoration took place, had lost out to Chicago in the competition for the world's fair, the so-called World's Columbian Exposition (1893), so as if to compensate it staged a five-day city-wide extravaganza culminating on Columbus Day itself. The event drew a million visitors and filled the streets with parades, festivals and tributes. Houses were extravagantly adorned, lamps lit up the night, businesses closed down for the day, and an eighty-four foot monument of Columbus was added to Central Park, a gift of Italians and Americans of Italian descent.[1]

Jews participated actively in the 1892 gala. The Committee of One Hundred that planned the celebration, seeking to begin the festivities with what the *Tribune* called "hearty thanksgiving to the Creator for having bestowed on this great Nation such a home as America to grow upon," invited Jews to inaugurate the celebration with special synagogue services on Saturday morning. The *Tribune* reported that services "in all the Hebrew synagogues in the town" would make "special reference to the occasion," and that in many of them "the preparations have been elaborate."[2]

This was also the week of *Sukkot* in New York, and by coincidence both Columbus' original landing and its 400th anniversary fell on Hoshanah Rabba, the seventh and last day of the festival. "The day on which the Jews ... in every part of the world were singing their hosannas," one contemporary historian pointed out, the cry "*Tierra, Tierra*" ("Land, Land") arose from the *Pinta*.[3] New York's chief rabbi,

81

Jacob Joseph, published a special prayer for the occasion (written by his assistant Julius Buchhalter), its flowery Hebrew text expressing gratitude not only for Columbus, "the first man in the New World," but also for the two Jews who, according to the prayer, accompanied him on his voyage. The prayer went on to pay tribute to America's subsequent role as a refuge for persecuted Jews, highlighted the nation's tradition of religious freedom and equality, praised George Washington, and closed with a blessing for President Benjamin Harrison and his government.[4]

The chief rabbi's prayer, which was widely disseminated,[5] embodied all three of the themes that, as we shall see, proved central to American Jewish thinking about Columbus. First, it directly linked his activities to Jewish history, in this case by pointing to Jews who supposedly travelled on his vessel. This served to legitimate the whole Jewish presence in the New World, allowing Jews to say, as it were, "we were here from the start." Second, the prayer associated Columbus with the freedoms that were so centrally important to American Jews, particularly freedom from persecution and freedom for religious minorities. It thus depicted America both as a refuge for immigrants and as a land of liberty and equality. Finally, the prayer used Columbus as a vehicle for expressing Jewish patriotism. It proudly pledged allegiance to the values that America stood for and invoked God's blessing upon the President and his administration.

Sermons delivered during the quatre-centennial celebration echoed these same themes. One was entitled "The Importance of Columbus' Discovery for the Jews"; another considered "The Achievements of Columbus for the Benefit of Mankind and the Jews in Particular." A well-publicized sermon by Rabbi Alexander Kohut of Temple Ahawath Chesed, one of the foremost traditional rabbis in New York and Professor of Talmud and Midrash at the Jewish Theological Seminary, actually argued that Columbus and the Jews had much in common. Both brought immeasurable benefit to the world, and both were denied their rightful inheritance, as others (in Columbus' case, Amerigo Vespucci) received credit for work they had done. Moreover, Jews, according to Kohut, had a special reason to express gratitude to God for Columbus, since he had "founded a haven of repose for our noble race . . . he discovered a country for wandering Israel as well as for others."

Cincinnati's Reform Jewish leader, Rabbi Isaac Mayer Wise, in a retrospective on the day, took note of the rhetorical excesses that his rabbinical colleagues fell prey to. "Columbus Day," he observed somewhat sardonically, "was celebrated in most all temples and synagogues in the land with special eclat; the structures were decorated with national flags[;] choirs and congregations sang the national songs; preachers delivered eloquent orations. A vast amount of patriotism was elaborated and consummated. . . . The outbursts of patriotism are extremely edifying to loyal citizens; the Columbus culte [sic] is less legitimate in the estimation of strict monotheists. . . ."[6]

Actually, the most significant American Jewish contribution to the national celebration of 1892 received only modest recognition at the time—although in the years ahead it would be remembered while everything else was forgotten. This was the scholarly research of Rabbi Meyer (Moritz) Kayserling, written up in several articles in 1892 and then two years later as a book. Kayserling (1829-1905), the rabbi of Budapest, had studied with the great German historian Leopold Ranke, and had written prolifically in many areas of Jewish history, specializing in Spanish and Portuguese Jewry and the Marranos.[7] Back in 1857, he had published a short article in which he first pointed to the role that Jews had played in the Spanish and Portuguese discoveries.[8] In 1891, he was commissioned by the American Jewish merchant Lazarus Straus and his diplomat son Oscar Solomon Straus to prepare a scholarly volume demonstrating the extent to which Jews shared in Columbus' enterprise. The result was *Christopher Columbus and the Participation of the Jews in the Spanish and Portuguese Discoveries.*

Oscar Straus' interest in demonstrating the compatibility of Americanism and Judaism was of long standing; he had himself published a volume in 1885 that purported to show "the influence of the Hebrew Commonwealth upon the Origin of Republican Government in the United States." His argument, drawing heavily on Puritan sources, was the by now familiar one that (in a phrase attributed to the British historian W.E.H. Lecky) "Hebrew mortar cemented the foundations of American democracy." More than just scholarship lay behind this claim, however, for as Professor Jerold Auerbach has persuasively shown, it was freighted with ideological baggage. Thanks to the book, "American Jews could not only demonstrate the inherent unity of the Jewish and America[n] traditions but also claim the Puritans as 'their' spiritual forbears."[9] The volume became the bible of those who embraced what might properly be called "the cult of American-Jewish synthesis." Something of this same spiritual quest seems to have sparked Straus' interest in making known the participation of Jews in Columbus' discovery.

The Great Mariner had evolved in the American mind into the embodiment of the national ideal, a symbol of American achievement, progress, and goodness.[10] By associating themselves with him, Jews would symbolically take on these virtues, yoking together their Americanism and their Judaism, and demonstrating the historical indispensability of Jews to the whole American enterprise. Precisely these claims, though not in so many words, were in fact made by the American Jewish Historical Society, which was founded in 1892, and over which Oscar Straus presided.

More immediately, Straus believed, as he admitted in a private letter to Kayserling, that if it could be historically proven that Jews had taken an active part in the discovery of America, "this fact would be an answer for all time to come to antisemitic tendencies in this country."[11] This was a most remarkable and revealing assumption. Although they rarely spoke of the problem in public, domestic antisemitism was already of substantial concern to American Jewish leaders. Conditions had been deteriorating for American Jews since the 1870s, and the Straus family had itself been the victim of social discrimination. In one memorable incident, several members of the family were refused admission by a hotel in Lakewood, N.J.; in response, Oscar's brother, Nathan Straus (the owner of the R.H. Macy department store), purchased land nearby and built the Lakewood Hotel, which he opened to Jews and Gentiles alike.[12] These sorts of personal encounters likely underlay Straus' strenuous efforts, throughout his life, to polish up the image of American Jews so that they might be better respected.

Beyond this, the letter to Kayserling reveals a common nineteenth-century belief that American Jews through their own positive actions and especially by spreading correct information about themselves, could stamp antisemitism out. The Kayserling mission, the founding of the American Jewish Historical Society, and a few years later the completion of the *Jewish Encyclopedia* all reflect this buoyantly optimistic point of view; they also help explain why all of these scholarly undertakings proved so popular in elite circles.[13] If only the record could be set straight, Straus and many of his generation believed, prejudice against Jews would disappear. All that Jewish scholars like Kayserling had to do was come up with the right facts and publicize them.

Kayserling certainly fulfilled his part of the bargain. His well-documented study disclosed a hitherto unknown[14] web of ties between Columbus and Jews or recent forced converts from Judaism (*conversos*), stretching from those who supplied him with maps, astronomical tables, and nautical instruments, to those who championed his cause before the Spanish crown, to those who, like the convert Luis de Santangel—the book's hero—actually supported Columbus' journey financially. The volume also listed four men "of Jewish stock" as having accompanied Columbus to the New World (actually, only one of them—the interpreter Luis de Torres, who had converted to Christianity not long before—was of certain Jewish descent.)

Most important of all, Kayserling showed that Columbus' reward was paid out of funds expropriated from Jews expelled from Spain in 1492, and that the same source—not the Queen's jewels, as popular myth had it, but her Jews—would defray the costs of his second voyage as well. Finally, Kayserling traced the spread of *conversos* to the New World, the persecutions they faced at the hands of the Inquisition, and the (inevitable) happy end: "the New World . . . was not merely a land rich in gold and silver mines, but also the land where the light of freedom first shone upon the adherents of Judaism."[15] An appendix consisting of thirty-six pages of untranslated documents from the Spanish archives rounded out the volume and gave it appropriate scholarly ballast.

Kayserling's volume was published in three languages (German, English and Hebrew), and its conclusions attracted wide notice.[16] While his researches had no discernible effect on the incidence of American antisemitism, they did influence most of Columbus' subsequent biographers.[17]

Naturally, the book earned its warmest reception in Jewish circles. Thus, during the 1905 celebrations of the 250th anniversary of Jewish settlement in the United States, it was cited repeatedly to prove that "the Jew has played an honorable and not undistinguished part in the history and development of the Western continent," and that "we, whose ancestors bore their share in the mission of Columbus . . . may well reckon ourselves as the first of Americans, bone of the bone and flesh of the flesh of Columbia." According to the scholar Joseph Jacobs (writing in 1910), the significance of Kayserling's book could "scarcely be overrated" suggesting as it did "the existence of a Jewish element in America from its very originings [sic]. The Jews preceded the Anglo-Saxon on American soil." On Columbus Day 1918, Rabbi Joseph Stolz of Chicago cited Kayserling yet again: "lest we forget . . . that even though there was a time when . . . Palestine harbored no Hebrews, there never was a time when white people were on American soil in anticipation of the Jews."[18]

In short, Kayserling's research validated the sense of American Jews that they had sunk deep roots in the country and had contributed mightily to its growth and welfare. In an era when most American Jews were newcomers, immigrants from Eastern Europe, and when even those born in America felt threatened both by antisemitism and by restrictions on further Jewish immigration, this reading of the nation's past could not have been more welcome.

Nothing in Meyer Kayserling's book so much as hinted at the idea that Columbus himself might have been a Jew. To the contrary, Kayserling criticized the explorer for his religious fanaticism and for his *lack* of sympathy toward Jews who were, after all, being expelled at the very moment he was setting out to sea.[19] Nor, so far as I can tell, did anyone else in 1892 suggest that Columbus was anything other than what he claimed to be—namely, a religious Catholic and a native of Genoa.

The idea that Columbus was a Jew arose instead in non-Jewish circles in Spain. The man who first promoted the idea was an aristocratic scholar named Don Garcia de la Riega, and his evidence consisted of documents (now believed to have been largely forged) that he claimed to have found in Pontevedra in Galicia. These contained the names of members of the Colon family, whom he associated with Columbus, and of the Fonterossa family whom he associated with Columbus' wife, and whose ancestors turned out to be Jewish. From these rather meager shards, de la Riega fashioned a highly original theory that purported to solve the many mysteries connected with Columbus' name, background, and life by arguing that Columbus was really a secret Jew, who had been born in Spain, not Genoa, and who had spent a lifetime concealing his identity.

De la Riega's theory had important political implications, for if he was correct, Spain and not Italy could claim the honor of having Columbus as a native son. Perhaps, too, there was some hope that this "discovery" might lead to an improvement in Spanish-American relations, damaged lately in the Spanish-American War. Whatever the case, Hispanophiles rushed to spread the good news. A variety of pamphlets were soon issued, including one, in 25,000 copies, circulated to governments, learned societies and distinguished personalities, that entreated them "to move heaven and earth" to make everyone aware that Columbus was in fact a Spaniard by birth.[20]

The theory that Columbus was not only a Spaniard but a closet Jew peaked during the decade of the 1930s, an era when (perhaps only coincidentally), the "Jewish question" was very much on the public's mind. A whole range of proofs was put forward, a few based on written evidence, most totally circumstantial, and some unabashedly racial. While it is impossible to review all of this evidence here,[21] it breaks down as follows:

First, there was the evidence based on Columbus' name, or names. "Colon" was a name held by many Jewish families, and among Italian Jews (as the historian Cecil Roth pointed out) the shift back and forth from "Colon" to "Colombo"—a shift that Columbus himself seems to have made several times—was "not only possible but invariable."[22] Yet there were also non-Jews by these names both in Spain and in Italy, so this evidence alone could not be considered conclusive.

Second, Columbus employed and enjoined upon his descendants a most unusual, mystical signature, written in the form of a triangle:

.S.
.S. A .S.
X M Y
Xpo   FERENS

According to the American Jewish numismatist and antiquarian, Maurice David, these letters decoded into "an abbreviation of the 'last confession' of the Jews and also a substitute for the Kaddish." This view has been widely (and properly) dismissed as utterly unverifiable.[23] Still, the encoded signature has heightened the aura of mystery surrounding Columbus, and helps to explain why the theory of his *converso* origins continues to elicit support today.[24]

Third, Columbus placed a cryptic monogram at the top left corner of most of his intimate letters. Could this be, as Maurice David suggested, "nothing more nor less than an old Hebrew greeting," an abbreviation of *baruch hashem*, blessed be the Lord? Many readers (myself among them) cannot see it, but once again the mystery cries out for explanation.

Fourth, Columbus' written prose sets a considerable puzzle: if the explorer was born in Genoa, why was his Italian so poor and his Castilian so good? Salvador de Madariaga, the great Spanish biographer of Columbus and perhaps the most important proponent of the theory that he was of Jewish descent, anchored his thesis on this point, hypothesizing that Columbus' parents were Spanish Jews who had departed for Genoa in the face of persecution and then "remained faithful to the language of their country of origin." More recent studies, however, propose an alternative hypothesis: that Columbus learned his

Spanish in Portugal where he was married, a conclusion buttressed by the fact that his Spanish betrays Portuguese characteristics. As for why he knew no Italian, these writers explain that it was then only the literary language of Genoa, whereas he spoke the local dialect, and may in any case in those days have been totally illiterate.[25]

Fifth, a bundle of circumstantial evidence links Columbus to Jews. *Item*: like many Spanish *conversos*, he and his family were highly secretive and took great pains to conceal their background—suggesting that they had something to hide. *Item*: the family's occupation, weaving, was frequently associated with Jews. *Item*: Columbus himself fraternized with Jews, had some knowledge of Jewish mystical sources, occasionally linked his experiences to events in ancient Jewish history, and even left a small legacy to a Jew.

Yet none of this by itself proves anything, and some of it may be better explained by the explorer's apocalyptic view of history and particularly by his lofty sense of himself as a divine messenger, the Christbearer (=Christopher) of a new age.[26] It may even be that he envisaged an important role for Jews in God's divine plan and so both embraced the remnants of Israel and sought to convert them. But this too is speculative. For although we know more about Columbus than about any other explorer of his day, many mysteries connected with his life remain unresolved.

I have left until last the so-called "racial" proofs of Columbus' Jewishness for they stand in a class by themselves. Here, for example, is Jacob Wasserman in his biography, *Columbus: Don Quixote of the Seas*:

> A certain soft-heartedness in Columbus is a Jewish trait, in the best and the worst sense of that adjective; Jewish, too, is his unmistakable inclination to find a sentimental solution for practical problems; Jewish, likewise, is his characteristic timidity in the face of far-reaching responsibilities—a timidity that springs from age-long fear of the irrevocable and of what has been decided from above. But what is *not* Jewish is his striking want of intelligence and practical capacity, and above all, that form of Don-Quixotry that consists in subjecting the mind to the dream of a perverted reality—a trait completely foreign to the Jewish character.[27]

The eminent Spanish historian, Salvador de Madariaga, went even farther—indeed, alarmingly so. Noting, for example, that Columbus evinced a keen attraction for gems and gold, he writes:

> The Jews have always experienced a curious fascination for gold and precious stones, forms of nature which, quite apart from their commercial value, are in deep harmony with the soul of Israel.

Madariaga also found evidence of Columbus' Jewishness in his "contractual sense, that attitude which sees every event of life as a transaction and expects and demands a definite *quid* for every *quo*." He even detected evidence of hidden Jewishness in Columbus' illicit relationship with Beatrice Enriquez, the mother of the mariner's illegitimate child, Fernando, and in Madariaga's view, herself a secret Jew. "The sexual morality of the Jews was of course different from that of the Christians," he blithely reports, ". . . in those days a Christian young woman who gave herself without marriage was almost certainly a good-for-nothing, [whereas] a Jewish girl who gave herself without marriage might very possibly be a thoroughly decent soul." Since, in Madariaga's version of events, the young, new-Christian Beatriz *was* a thoroughly decent soul, she agreed to do "what an 'old-Christian' woman would not have done"—she slept with him.[28]

Now, Wasserman was an identifying Jew and Madariaga was something of a philo-Semite, yet they—and many others who have labeled Columbus a Jew—consciously or unconsciously promote the myth that Jews differ radically in their personal characteristics, their values, and their mores from those among whom they live, and that they are unable no matter how hard they try fully to conceal their origins. The thinly veiled message here is one that antisemites have propounded for centuries: that no matter what loyalties a Jew may proclaim, and regardless of whether (like Columbus) he publicly and privately professes his devotion to the Church, he remains both at heart and in behavior a child of Israel. Many an innocent Spaniard was targeted by the Inquisition on precisely these grounds.

It is, moreover, but one small step from this fantasy of an inherent Jewishness to an even more dangerous corollary: that Jews, operating illicitly and sometimes under the guise of another faith, are engaged in a gigantic conspiracy for their own benefit. Simon Wiesenthal, the great Nazi hunter whose familiarity with antisemitic canards is beyond question, has unfortunately fallen into this very trap in his version of the Columbus story, *Sails of Hope*. According to Wiesenthal, Columbus (whom he considers likely to have been a *converso*) embarked on his first voyage westward for a secret purpose: to discover the lands settled and ruled by the Lost Ten Tribes of Israel so that they might serve as a refuge for Jews being expelled from Spain. (That the American Indians were themselves the descendants of the Lost Ten Tribes was once a staple myth not only among Jews but among many Christians as well.)

On the surface, this theory—Wiesenthal calls it, in one place, "Operation New World"—seems to clear up several mysteries: why Columbus maintained so many Jewish contacts, why Jews and *conversos* supported his enterprise financially, and why he brought along a Hebrew-speaking interpreter. Like all conspiracy theories, however, it ignores both simpler alternative explanations and a mass of inconvenient evidence, including, in this case, the explorer's own writings that detail his materialistic and millenarian hopes, as well as his obvious intention to exploit his discoveries for the benefit of Spain.

In addition, the Wiesenthal theory requires an immense leap of faith, since there is no evidence from any source that Spanish Jews wanted to secure a refuge with the Lost Ten Tribes in "Asia"; it was easier to go underground or to move to Portugal or to Turkey. All that Wiesenthal does, in the end, is to encourage an idea that in other circumstances he would be the first to refute: the idea that Jews are disloyal, conniving, and notwithstanding any patriotic claims they might make, out only to help their own.[29]

To their credit, most Jewish scholars greeted the theory of Columbus' Jewish origins with considerable skepticism. Neither the major Jewish encyclopedias nor the major surveys of American Jewish history accepted the claim at face value. For the most part, they laid the evidence out in an objective manner and attributed the theory to Spanish historians.[30] The most widely used mid-twentieth century Hebrew school textbook in American Jewish history, Rabbi Lee J. Levinger's *A History of the Jews in the United States*, took its cue from these scholars. While it devoted three long paragraphs to Columbus, it concluded that the evidence for his being a Jew was insufficient. "We should be very proud to claim this great explorer and intrepid spirit as a Jew, if the facts warranted it," Levinger admitted, "but it is not possible to do so without real proof. . . ."[31]

A rather pathetic pamphlet, published by the self-styled founder of the Sephardic press in America, Moise S. Gadol, attempted, in 1941, to revitalize the theory that "Christopher Columbus was a Spanish-Jew," but its aims in setting forth this "important history" were all too transparent:

> Therefore, all Jews, descendants of Cristobal Colon [Columbus], should be respected by all other nationalities living in this great Continent. In this New World there is no room for anti-semitism. The Jews must be treated with equality in commemoration of the discoverer CRISTOBAL COLON THE JEW.[32]

Cecil Roth, the noted Anglo-Jewish historian, also defended the theory, influenced both by Madariaga and by his own study of the behavior of the Marranos. He even hinted that he could identify Columbus' real Jewish name.[33]

But once Samuel Eliot Morison, in his magisterial biography of Christopher Columbus, published in 1942, derided the theory—his book even included an index entry which reads "Jews, C.C. not one"—the theory's last vestiges of scholarly support crumbled. Without mincing words, Morrison insisted that "there is no more reason to doubt that Christopher Columbus was a Genoese-born Catholic Christian, steadfast in his faith and proud of his native city, than to doubt that George Washington was a Virginian-born Anglican of English race, proud of being an American."[34] Even Roth in an article written just before his death for the *Encyclopaedia Judaica* came close to conceding the point: "The mystery regarding Columbus' origins is largely the outcome of his own mendacity," he explained, "and as a result it is equally impossible to exclude or to confirm the hypothesis that he was descended from a Jewish or ex-Jewish family."[35]

The 500th anniversary of Columbus' voyage has, naturally, led to a flurry of new articles on the question of his Jewishness, but with a revealing contemporary twist. Thus, in "Was the Discoverer of America Jewish?" *Moment* magazine reminds its readers that Columbus' "discovery" was "disastrous" for the native population, leading to millions of deaths, and that, in addition, the explorer introduced into the New World the scourge of slavery. "Do we really want to claim Columbus?" *Moment*'s editors ask.[36] And Professor Judith Laikin Elkin, writing in *Hadassah* has made a similar point:

> The search for Jewish ancestry for Columbus is particularly untimely now, when Native Americans are drawing our

attention to the genocide that paved the way for the creation of our New World.

To the question, "Columbus: Was He or Wasn't He?" she responds: "Who cares?"[37]

There is, however, at least one good reason to care about the century-long obsession with Columbus' putative Jewish past and his indubitable Jewish associations, and that is for whatever clues it may provide to the way American Jews think about themselves. For it is a remarkable fact that among America's ethnic and religious groups only one, the Jews, has linked itself to so many of the nation's founding myths. These myths—the Indians, were the Lost Ten Tribes; the Puritans were "Hebraic" to the core; Columbus was aided by Jews and may even have been one himself—have precious little to do with the real history and significance of the Indians, the Puritans or Columbus. But they do speak volumes about American Jews, their loyalties, and their insecurities.

NOTES

An earlier and shorter version of this paper was published in *Commentary*, November 1992.

1. Claudia L. Bushman, *America Discovers Columbus* (Hanover, NH: University Press of New England, 1992).

2. *New York Tribune*, October 8, 1892, 1.

3. Moritz Kayserling, *Christopher Columbus and the Participation of the Jews in the Spanish and Portuguese Discoveries* (New York: Hermon Press, 1968 [orig. ed. 1894]), 91.

4. Mosheh Starkman [Khizquni], "Tefilah Le-Yovel Ha-400 Le-Giluy 'Ameriqah'," *Bitzaron* 37:3 (January 1958), 129-31; Jacob Kabakoff, *Seekers and Stalwarts: Essays and Studies on American Hebrew Literature and Culture* (Jerusalem: Rubin Mass, 1978), 267-268 [in Hebrew]. I am grateful to Professor Kabakoff for providing me with a copy of this item. On the career of Jacob Joseph, see Abraham J. Karp, "New York Chooses a Chief Rabbi," *Publications of the American Jewish Historical Society*, 44 (March 1955): 129-198.

5. J. Kabakoff, *Seekers and Stalwarts*, 267, claims that the prayer was published in both Hebrew and English in the *New York Herald*. It also appeared in the Yiddish press.

6. Bushman, *America Discovers Columbus*, 168; J.D. Eisenstein, *Ozar Zikhronothai: Autobiography and Memoirs* [in Hebrew] (New York: the author, 1929), 76; *American Israelite*, October 27, 1892. For other accounts, see especially the *New York Tribune*, October 9, 1892; *American Israelite*, October 20, 1892; and *Jewish Messenger*, October 14-28, 1892.

7. Cecil Roth, "Kayserling, Meyer," *Encyclopedia Judaica* 10 (1972): col. 855-856; Joseph Jacobs, "Meyer Kayserling," *Publications of the American Jewish Historical Society* 16 (1907): 205-207.

8. Meyer Kayserling, "Die Portugiesischen Entdeckung und Eroberungen in Beziehung zu den Juden," *Monatschrift fuer Geschichte und Wissenschaft des Judentums* 7 (1857): 433-36.

9. Jerold S. Auerbach, *Rabbis and Lawyers: The Journey from Torah to Constitution* (Bloomington, IN: Indiana University Press, 1990), 14.

10. Bushman, *America Discovers Columbus*, 158-59.

11. Oscar Straus to Meyer Kayserling, March 11, 1892, as quoted in Naomi Cohen, *A Dual Heritage: The Public Career of Oscar S. Straus* (Philadelphia: Jewish Publication Society, 1969), 71.

12. David de Sola Pool, "Oscar Straus," *American Jewish Year Book* 33 (1931-32): 148.

13. Shuly Rubin Schwartz, *The Emergence of Jewish Scholarship in America: The Publication of the* Jewish Encyclopedia (Cincinnati: Hebrew Union College Press, 1991), 16; Jonathan D. Sarna, *JPS: The Americanization of Jewish Culture* (Philadelphia: Jewish Publication Society, 1989), 24,93; Nathan M. Kaganoff, "AJHS at 90: Reflections on the History of the Oldest Ethnic Historical Society in America," *American Jewish History* 71:4 (June 1982), 472-473.

14. George A. Kohut in *Publications of the American Jewish Historical Society* 33 (1934): 36 notes several writers whose works anticipated Kayserling to some degree, but without the archival sources that he brought to bear on the subject.

15. M. Kayserling, *Christopher Columbus and the Participation of the Jews in the Spanish and Portuguese Discoveries* (New York: Hermon Press, 1968).

16. Kayserling also wrote the articles on "America, Discovery of" and "Columbus, Christopher, and the Jews" in the *Jewish Encyclopedia* (1901-6), where he summarized his researches; see also Schwartz, *The Emergence of Jewish Scholarship in America*, 113- 114.

17. Even Werner Sombart, who felt that Jews were exaggerating their claims ("it is as though . . . Columbus and the rest were but managing directors for Israel") still relied on Kayserling; see his *The Jews and Modern Capitalism* [1911], translated by M. Epstein (New York: Collier Books, 1962), 50-51, 335 n. 11. For a recent treatment that continues to cite Kayserling, see John Noble Wilford, *The Mysterious History of Columbus* (New York: Knopf, 1991), 288.

18. *The Two Hundred and Fiftieth Anniversary of the Settlement of the Jews in the United States* (New York: New York Cooperative Society, 1906), 48, 63 [also reprinted as volume 14 of the *Publications of the American Jewish Historical Society*]; Jacob Joseph, "Charles Gross," *Publications of the American Jewish Historical Society* 19 (1910): 192; "Proceedings of the Jewish Historical Society of Illinois, October 12, 1918" reprinted in Hyman L. Meites, *History of the Jews of Chicago* (Chicago: Chicago Jewish Historical Society, 1990 [orig. ed. 1924]), 778.

19. Kayserling, *Columbus*, 80.

20. Henry Vignaud, "Columbus A Spaniard and a Jew," *American Historical Review* 18 (April 1913): 505-512.

21. For a more exhaustive review of the evidence, see Charles Alperin, "Christopher Columbus—A Jew?" *Midstream* 25 (March 1979): 35-47.

22. Cecil Roth, *Personalities and Events in Jewish History* (Philadelphia: Jewish Publication Society, 1953), 203-4.

23. Maurice David, *Who Was Columbus?* (New York: Research publishing Co., 1933), 103; Roth, *Personalities and Events*, 209.

24. A more recent theory links the signature to Columbus' apocalypticism, see Wilford, *The Mysterious History of Columbus*, 224.

25. Salvador de Madariaga, *Christopher Columbus* (New York: Macmillan, 1940), 50-53; Wilford, *The Mysterious History of Columbus*, 62.

26. Wilford, *The Mysterious History of Columbus*, 215-234, offers a convenient summary of recent evidence.

27. Jacob Wasserman, *Columbus: Don Quixote of the Seas*, trans. Eric Sutton (Boston: Little Brown, 1930), 151. Wasserman was an important German-Jewish novelist, who seems to have read some aspects of his own life as a Jew into Columbus. His account apparently had a considerable impact on Madariaga.

28. Madariaga, *Christopher Columbus*, 90, 136, 159-60. In *attacking* the theory that Columbus was a Jew, a recent biographer, John Stewart Collis, employs similar evidence: "One can easily draw up a whole list of traits about anyone and call them Jewish, though they could apply equally well to many races stretching from Ireland to India. But when a man is found lacking in the main characteristic of a given race, we cannot easily suppose that he belongs to that race. The Jews are realists to a man; they know the composition of things; they know the score as we say; they are always on the *qui vive* against being deceived, and they do not deceive themselves. Their grasp of reality is not canny so much as positively uncanny. And, as we shall see throughout the whole story of Columbus, it was precisely in this characteristic that he was totally lacking." John Stewart Collis, *Christopher Columbus* (New York: Stein and Day, 1976), 30-31.

29. Simon Wiesenthal, *Sails of Hope: The Secret Mission of Christopher Columbus* (New York: Macmillan, 1973), quotes are from 53, 60.

30. Abraham A. Neuman's article, "Columbus, Christopher" in the *Universal Jewish Encyclopedia* 3 (1941): 306-310 is the most sympathetic to the theory; the unsigned article in the same volume on "David, Maurice" speaks of his theory having been proved "conclusively" (487).

31. Lee J. Levinger, *A History of the Jews in the United States* (New York: Union of American Hebrew Congregations, 1949), 28- 29.

32. Moise S. Gadol, *Christopher Columbus was a Spanish Jew* (New York: the author, 1941), copy in the library of the American Jewish Historical Society, Waltham, MA.

33. Cecil Roth, "Who Was Columbus?" *Menorah Journal* 28 (1940): 279-95, reprinted in Roth, *Personalities and Events in Jewish History* (Philadelphia: Jewish Publication Society, 1953), 192-211.

34. Samuel Eliot Morison, *Admiral of the Ocean Sea: A Life of Christopher Columbus* (Boston: Little Brown, 1942), 7, 206, 677.

35. Cecil Roth, "Columbus, Christopher," *Encyclopaedia Judaica* 5 (1972): col. 756-757; see also Salo Baron's review of the literature in *Social and Religious History of the Jews* 13 (New York: Columbia University Press, 1969): 132-134, 376-379.

36. Newton Frohlich, "Was the Discoverer of America Jewish?" *Moment* 16 (December 1991): 35-43.

37. Judith Laikin Elkin, "Columbus: Was He or Wasn't He?" *Hadassah Magazine* 73 (January 1992): 49-50.

The Other Side of the Story: Indigenous Interpretation of Contact with Europeans

Dale Stover

In his book, *Stolen Continents: The Americas Through Indian Eyes Since 1492*, which was published in the quincentennial year of 1992, Ronald Wright sets out a dramatic hermeneutic stage for our topic. He writes:

> Within decades of Columbus's landfall, most of these [indigenous] people were dead and their world barbarously sacked by Europeans. The plunderers settled in America, and it was they, not the original people, who became known as Americans.
>
> Conventional history, even when it acknowledges the enormity of this assault, has led us to assume that it is finished, irrevocable; that America's peoples are extinct or nearly so; that they were so primitive and died so quickly, they had nothing to say. . . . For five centuries we have listened only to the history of the winners. We have been talking to ourselves. It is time to hear the other side of the story that began in 1492 and continues to this day.[1]

With that introduction, one might assume that contemporary scholarship could proceed to consider cases of indigenous commentary on contact with Europeans. Unfortunately, the hermeneutic situation is not so simple as that. There are certain dilemmas which confound the possibility of straightforward understanding taking place. There is

97

the issue of the intelligibility of indigenous discourse outside the social and symbolic world of that particular people. Usually, the "we" who are the offspring of European-derived discourse frame this issue as the problem of *their* intelligibility rather than perceiving it as a shortcoming in the versatility and perspicacity of *our* discursive resources.

There is also the dilemma of attunement to indigenous discourse. For those of us who are the modern inheritors of the European side of this encounter, the indigenous voice represents the story of the Other, that over against which the European "discoverers" defined themselves. Since European self-identity is at stake in listening to this Other, attunement to indigenous discourse may be limited to a hearing which remains securely within the familiar definitions of Self and Other.

A very different attunement, one which is open to hearing indigenous voices as speaking words of value within a common human discourse, would represent a daring hermeneutic adventure and might entail the deconstruction of the categories of both the indigenous Other and the European-derived Self. Of course, it is possible that such a deconstruction may turn out to be deceptive, remaining completely within the European discourse and never transcending to an actual engagement with indigenous discourse. In such a case, the interpreter assumes a scholarly perspective outside of the field of European discourse in order to deconstruct it, but the supposed meta-perspective remains within the mythological boundaries of European discourse which are, in fact, identical to the borders of scholarly discourse. A real deconstruction of Self and Other can only take place within a discourse which embraces the Other as simply other, which includes both sides of the story.

The hermeneutic challenge of hearing the indigenous side of the story is the stretching, enlarging, and reframing of European discourse in order to embrace intelligibly what presents itself as novel and strange and to achieve an attunement to indigenous voices as weighing, formulating, and expressing the existential concerns of a common humanity. For understanding to blossom, a similar movement must take place on the indigenous side of the mutual field of discourse. Because such a field of discourse did not become established in the fifteenth and sixteenth centuries nor in the centuries following, mutual understanding remains problematic in 1992. The issues of intelligibility and attunement continue to impede understanding, so that it is astonishing to find so much "we" and "they" referencing in the present situation.

An examination of three contemporary works which have made notable attempts to reconnoitre the hermeneutic frontier between indigenous and European-oriented discourse may serve to illuminate the tangled character of past and present interpretive efforts. These three interpreters represent quite separate hermeneutic enterprises, each with certain heuristic benefits and each with specific interpretive limitations. After consideration of these three approaches, an attempt will be made toward the reframing of the hermeneutic situation to foster a more genuinely mutual and inclusive field of discourse in which both European-oriented and indigenous voices can be heard and understood.

RONALD WRIGHT'S RESISTANCE NARRATIVES

Ronald Wright, from whom we have already heard, serves as the first of our three interpretive guides. Wright speaks of most history as being myth, "an arrangement of the past, whether real or imagined, in patterns that resonate with a culture's deepest values and aspirations."[2] He also refers to the West's myth of discovery as a transformation of "historical crimes into glittering icons."[3] The history of both sides of the story is mythic, claims Wright, with one being triumphalist and the other centered around the theme of resistance.[4]

A chief virtue of Wright's book is its pointing to what he terms "a remarkable body of *post*-Columbian native documents" which have been newly brought forth "from centuries of oblivion in archives and collections."[5] Wright selects five indigenous societies to represent the other side of the story since 1492 and conceives of his book as telling this story. "My narrative," he writes, "is a kind of mortar linking fragmentary inscriptions."[6]

Wright styles the other side of the story as the tale of 500 years of resistance. He connects the early decades after 1492, the time of conquest, with resistance activities which he believes lay tracks all the way to the present, so that "the murder of Atawallpa in 1533 and the violence of today's Shining Path are parts of the same story."[7] The five societies Wright chooses are "the Aztecs of Mexico, the Maya of Guatemala and Yucatan, the Incas of Peru, the Cherokees of the southern United States, and the Iroquois of the Great Lakes."[8] He claims that these five represent a story with 500 years continuity because they "have kept alive their languages, religions, certain arts and sciences, and countless intangibles of culture against all odds."[9] Wright claims that these five "are living cultures, defining and defending places in the contemporary world."[10] However, Wright is silent as to why he, rather than a representative from one of these five societies, is writing the book, and he is silent as to how agreeable the five peoples may be to his interpretive effort. In any case, he does clearly cast himself in the role of hermeneutic advocate on their behalf, presuming to serve them with the industry of his investigative scholarship and his forceful rhetoric.

Of the five societies Wright selects, three of them—the Aztecs, Maya, and Incas—are primarily affected by the Spanish conquest, and it is to the specifics of their stories as presented by Wright that our attention is drawn by the theme of this Symposium. In each of the three cases Wright attacks the European myth of conquest which claimed that spectacular victories over these indigenous empires by small numbers of conquistadors resulted from indigenous deficiency in valor and physical courage, and that they were cowed by the fierceness of the conquistadors or by thinking them to be gods. Wright cites much counter-evidence, beginning in 1502 when Columbus's ship encounters a Maya seagoing canoe and the Spanish account reports that the crew, on the orders of their master, "indicated arrogantly to our men that they should make way, and made threats when they offered resistance."[11] Wright comments that, "far from mistaking the strangers for gods, these Mayas—the first to meet Europeans—ordered them to stand aside."[12]

Wright lays out the history of conquest in the three instances of Aztec, Maya, and Inca, and he gives account of the admirable warrior qualities and efforts of each of the three. He also emphasizes the strategic role of European diseases in incapacitating the leadership and resistance capabilities in each of the three conquest histories. Wright calls European disease "a political assassination squad, removing kings, generals, and seasoned advisors at the very time they were needed most."[13]

In the course of charting resistance movements in each of the three defeated societies, Wright describes their views of the nature of time as a critical factor in each society's style of resistance. These accounts are, perhaps, the most successful of Wright's attempts to situate his perspective within the other side of the story. In the case of the Aztec story, Wright notes that an Aztec calendar round of 52 years had begun in 1507, and that soon after, probably in 1511, the first reports of Europeans arrived at the capital. Wright suggests that the subsequent events of Cortes's appearance, the arrival of smallpox, the fall of the capital, the burning of Aztec priests in the fires of the Inquisition, and economic chaos convinced the people "that this Calendar Round would be the last, they they were living through the end of the world."[14] Beginning in 1533 a series of three prophets arose attacking the Catholic friars, eventually identifying them as demons from the stars, apocalyptic beings accompanying the end.[15] When the close of the fifty-two years did not bring the apocalypse, Wright notes that syncretism replaced apocalyptic rejection of European reality. He describes this syncretism as "a way of encoding the values of a conquered culture within a dominant culture," in a manner which "would allow the Franciscans to think they had succeeded—and allow the Aztecs to think they had survived."[16]

Syncretism hardly sounds like resistance, although Wright presents a very interesting story, which ties together the vision of the Virgin Mary to Juan Diego at the site of the ruins of the main shrine for Tonantzin-Coatlicue in 1531, the writing of the *Cantare Mexicanos* in the 1560s and 1570s, the use of psilocybin mushrooms as sacred hallucinogens, the unearthing of the statue of Tonantzin-Coatlicue in Mexico City on August 13, 1790, and the declaration by Servando Teresa de Mier in 1794 that Quetzalcoatl was really Saint Thomas the Apostle.[17] The upshot of Fray Servando's story was that Mexico had been Christian before Spain was, that Tonantzin-Coatlicue was actually the Virgin Mary, and that, in Servando's words, "The Spaniards and the missionaries, who saw the devil everywhere, had bedeviled everything."[18] In this way, the Spaniards were seen as blameworthy and the native traditions could be gratefully embraced, and so syncretism might be seen as resistance of a sort.

Unlike the cases of the Maya and the Inca, Wright's description of syncretism in Mexico claims that, "The Mexica Aztecs ceased to exist as a people during the colonial period, while simultaneously a new people, both Aztec and Spanish, came painfully into being."[19] The painfulness of resistance in the form of syncretism is reflected in Wright's telling of the story of the Mexican Revolution, 1911-1919, and the heroism of Emiliano Zapata. Although Zapata was dishonorably slain by government treachery, Wright notes that in this period *indigenismo* (Indianism) was deeply imprinted upon subsequent Mexican culture.[20]

The Maya, Wright tells us, marked time in katuns, twenty-year units. A full cycle of the calendar was 269 years, or thirteen katuns. Wright claims that the Maya maintained their equanimity in the face of Spanish conquest by categorizing it together with previous invasions. They had survived those, and they would survive this one. Wright describes how the Maya "merged pre-Columbian and post-Columbian history to create 'prophecy-history,'"[21] which gave them reassurance of the continuity of their Maya reality and the belief that Spanish rule would eventually run out of time.[22]

Wright tracks Maya resistance in the Yucatan and in Guatemala through to the twentieth century. He describes the Caste War of the nineteenth century, and he cites Victoria Bricker who wrote in 1981 that this was "without question the most successful Indian revolt in New World history."[23] This was a war between the Maya and the Ladinos, who were comprised of European settlers and mestizos. It began in January 1847, was nearly won by the Maya in 1848, and was lost by 1850, although the Maya state of The Speaking Cross survived in the jungle of Yucatan until the Mexican invasion of 1901.

Wright's description of resistance in Guatemala claims that it is "the most tragic country in the Americas."[24] He highlights recent times by reference to Rigoberta Menchu's 1982 autobiography. He quotes from an interview with her in 1990 in which the topic of the quincentenary of Columbus's arrival is raised. "The celebration of Columbus is for us an insult. . . . Our peoples have struggled, through sacrifice, through misery, for all these five hundred years. Who would celebrate their own colonization?"[25]

The Inca, notes Wright, tracked history according to a succession of ages, each of which ended through a cataclysmic period called a *pachakuti*, "an overturning of the world."[26] Wright describes how the arrival of smallpox and the Spanish were interpreted as a *pachakuti*. Wright explains that the Inca world was a system of complementary opposites, so that a *pachakuti* was not simply a chaotic change, but a reversal in polarity. It could be expected that a subsequent *pachakuti* would again reverse the fundamental polarity of cosmic order, in which case the Europeans would be out of power. Wright insists the peoples of the Andes are still expecting that next *pachakuti*.[27]

Wright traces Inca resistance through successive rebellions. We learn that while Simon Bolivar may have helped end Spanish rule in South America in the eighteenth century, Boliver's "'liberalism' . . . had no room for Incas."[28] Wright notes the birth of *indigenismo* in Peru during the aftermath of the War of the Pacific (1879-1883), and he links its cultural path to José María Arguedas, "whose work is widely regarded as indigenismo's highest literary expression."[29] While Peru has attempted to deny that indigenous people exist in the twentieth century, officially replacing the word *indio* with the term *campesino* (peasant),[30] Arguedas and others collect old Inca myths still circulating among the indigenous people which tell about waiting for the next *pachakuti*.[31]

Wright's hermeneutic intention of telling the other side of the story appears designed to raise consciousness on the part of Europeanized readers. His effort has a strong iconoclastic bent in the style of an investigative reporter producing an exposé which presents counter-evidence to the prevailing assumptions. Wright does this very effectively, and his work could be considered genuinely valuable and even, perhaps, necessary in order for a fundamental transformation to take place in the discursive encounter between indigenous and immigrant peoples.

At the same time, Wright's effort has limitations and may be seen as falling short of the hermeneutic process required for bringing about a common field of discourse embracing both sides of the story. For one thing, there is no serious reflection on the nature of Europeanized discourse or on Wright's own investment in this work. In place of this, there seems to be a polemical intent to reverse the character of Europeanized discourse, to see it as defective or wrong and in need of revision. Wright appears to cast himself as the opponent of what he unreflectingly takes to be the ruling mode of Europeanized discourse. This approach fosters polarization of the "stories" rather than rapprochement.

Wright's presumption to speak for the indigenous side of the story results in his own voice dominating the discourse, and it shows itself to be an ideological Western voice. This is covert paternalism. The reader is better informed in some respects, but he or she is still on the outside of indigenous discourse. Wright's one-sided effort to bring indigenous reality closer to Europeanized discourse tends to flatten differences among indigenous peoples and between indigenous and European-oriented world-views. While Wright provides sketches of indigenous cosmologies, his text remains itself largely within the field of Europeanized discourse with its themes of economic progress, colonization, nationalism, revolution, political reform, social justice, and ecological concern, and the reader may have no sense of having encountered a more shamanic understanding of reality. The question is whether Wright helps the Europeanized reader to understand the otherness of indigenous discourse or whether otherness is being inappropriately diminished, so that otherness becomes only a matter of being on the wrong historical side of political power.

LAWRENCE SULLIVAN'S SYSTEMATIC MYTHOLOGY

Lawrence Sullivan, our next interpretive guide, brings the issue of otherness into clearer focus. Sullivan's book, published in 1988, is *Icanchu's Drum: An Orientation to Meaning in South American Religions.* As the title indicates, Sullivan focuses on South America and on religion as a way to uncover the meaning of otherness. He notes that "the ideology of conquest permeates every image we possess of the people of the New world, and, since the Enlightenment that occurred during the Age of Exploration, has even shaped the way we think about knowledge."[32] This implies that the non-indigenous scholar has a personal stake in demythologizing the Age of Exploration, and Sullivan suggests that "the alienation from symbolic meaning so aptly illustrated by the modern social sciences may originate precisely in their avoidance of any serious confrontation with the realities of the many cultural mythologies that have flooded Western awareness since the Age of Discovery."[33] Sullivan's stress on "symbolic meaning" indicates that he is not as historically obsessed as Ronald Wright. Historical approaches can have an objectivizing, distancing effect, whereas Sullivan has his hopes set on a close engagement with indigenous discourse which will result in a transformation of his own understanding. "We must at some point confront and even reimagine whatever is real in our own world through the imagery provided by South American cultures."[34]

Nineteenth-century investigators of South American religions, says Sullivan, "overemphasized the seemingly bizarre and prompted comparative study of sensational themes. . . . These themes constitute how we know South American people and, therefore, they continue to preoccupy contemporary researchers."[35] Sullivan implies that an incalculable potency is latent in the otherness of South American symbolic images, which he calls "appearances" in a subsequent sentence. "The startling appearances of South American religious life can transform the ways we think about ourselves, others, and our world, just as they did when South American and European peoples first encountered one another."[36]

What Sullivan presents is an erudite, elegant, and encyclopedic entrée into the unfamiliar world of South American mythological understanding, *i.e.*, into the otherness of indigenous belief systems. He begins with a survey of South American cosmologies,[37] which leads into a consideration of myths about multiple epochs with accompanying destructive catastrophes.[38] His theory regarding the relationship of a catastrophic "fall" of the cosmos to the preceding primordial state of being and to the subsequent historical time may be his most valuable contribution toward a significant encounter with the meaning of South American traditions. Primordial being, Sullivan claims, was characterized by immediacy and absoluteness.[39] The problematic of primordial being was the lack of boundaries, of differentiation, of periodicity, and of transformational processes, so it was necessary that "primordial states of affairs had to come to a close through withdrawal, disappearance, or destruction."[40]

Sullivan sees the destruction of primordial reality as opening the way for symbolic meaning to life, since the primordium as such "cannot point beyond itself."[41] The details of the catastrophe myth show how the creative force of primordial being produces from its dismembered parts the modes and structures of an ordered cosmos within which human life may flourish. "The piecemeal state of primordial being ends the univocal world and creates the puzzle of multivalent existence and symbolic life."[42]

Sullivan's handling of this mythological transformation of primordial powers is brilliantly nuanced as can be seen in his treatment of the role of chaos. "Some form or other of primal chaos can become a definitive part of every image that is bounded and knowable; the chaos that brought an end to absolutely manifest being rings the contours of every comprehensible experience."[43] In this post-catastrophe world symbols play the key role; they "make life holy, ambiguous, paradoxical, and significant."[44] With this groundwork in place, Sullivan hopes to have legitimated his symbolic interpretation of the whole corpus of South American mythology.

Sullivan's mastery of the ethnographic maze of the otherness of South American diversity deserves acknowledgement, but this achievement includes some limits and concerns. Sullivan has treated the whole of South American mythology as though it exhibited a genuine coherence. He understands himself to be constructing a "morphology of South American religious life" which, he writes, is "an order of relationships among religious phenomena based on their symbolic forms and meaning."[45] In this aim of displaying a symbolic coherence for the whole there is a danger of discounting differences among the myths of various traditions and counting each as merely a variant of the same theme. When individual myths are considered only in relation to the architectonic structure of the whole range of South American mythology and not in connection with the mythological traditions of particular peoples, only the presumed "big picture" can be expected to emerge.

Sullivan's concentration on the entire corpus of South American mythology results in this corpus taking on the appearance of a unified text, and his insistence on finding symbolic coherence in the "text" gives the impression that he is expounding a sort of systematic "theology" of South American religion. This is a fascinating enterprise, and it may have some value, but pitfalls also abound. An effort to systematize tends to place the scholar in the role of the knowing subject arranging the elements of that which is known. This effort to know may become infected with concern to control and to domesticate the other within the familiar discourse of the knower, so that the scholar, in effect, manipulates the mapping of the myths to create a synthesis which is meaningful, *i.e.*, acceptable, to the scholar's own mythological outlook. In this way a scholar falls short of a real entry into the otherness of the indigenous world and only appropriates images from it.

Sullivan's ensnarement within his own systematizing mythology is evident in his treatment of the concept of supreme being. He notes that this concept is not a frequent one in South American myth, yet he insists that:

> the concept is crucial to students of religion, for it helps them gauge the outermost parameter of the religious imagination. Descriptions of supreme beings are culturally creative metastatements about the nature of creativity itself; these sublime images provide information about the subtlest powers and the most rarified possibilities of the religious imagination.[46]

It seems evident that Sullivan is preoccupied with a schema of religious conceptualization which possesses *a priori* a scale of sophistication for the "religious imagination" and which mandates categories such as supreme being quite apart from, or even in some opposition to, the mythological evidence. This indicates that Sullivan is pursuing some hermeneutic agenda other than that of encountering the particular truth of South American religious traditions.

A significant clue to Sullivan's hermeneutic intention is evident in his description of South America as "a black hole in the knowledge of the 'modern' world," and he asserts that "the religious life of South America, more than any other area, is unknown."[47] Sullivan seems to see South America as offering the greatest possible scope for the imaginative creativity of the scholar, as representing an opportunity to create a whole symbolic universe in a heretofore unspoiled mythological landscape. Sullivan's South America apparently holds special fascination for a scholar of religious images because it is the most other. Sullivan's systematizing approach runs the risk of playing the role of intellectual conquistador, searching in South America for the treasure trove of not-yet-discovered riches—in this case, the wealth of the "religious imagination." While Sullivan looks very searchingly at the otherness of South American religious traditions, his apolitical and ahistorical scholarship of the mythological corpus he encounters is flawed to the extent that it is overdetermined by the symbolic concerns of Western religious discourse.

MICHAEL TAUSSIG'S DEMYTHOLOGIZED SHAMANISM

Our third author, Michael Taussig, takes us on a yet different path toward the otherness of indigenous discourse by eschewing systematizing scholarship and offering instead a deliberately unmethodical method which he identifies as "montage," and which he has appropriated in significant respects from Walter Benjamin.[48] The idiosyncratic character of Taussig's hermeneutic approach is already suggested by the title of his book, *Shamanism, Colonialism, and the Wild Man: A Study in Terror and Healing*, published in 1987. He also turns to South America, Sullivan's "black hole," where he focuses upon the Putumayo region, located along the southern border of modern Columbia where it meets Ecuador and Peru; and he looks, not directly at the Age of Exploration, but at a period of intense colonial exploitation in the late nineteenth and early twentieth centuries. He notes what he calls "Hernán Pérez de Quesada's mad sweep through the jungles of the Caquetá and Putumayo in 1541 in search of El Dorado," and then declares that it is:

> startling to rediscover the language and imagery of the conquest of the New World in the sixteenth century, reactivated not by gold or by the story of El Dorado, but by quinine and rubber in the late nineteenth. Those European and North American booms for the raw materials of the rain forests resurrected in even more exaggerated form the heroic mythology of the earlier epoch and embedded it in the culture of the trading relationship.[49]

It is to the rain forest and to capitalist presence there that Taussig turns, and, unlike our two previous interpreters, his reflections on what he calls "the politics of epistemic murk and the fiction of the real,"[50] are informed by his having lived for some years among the people of whom he writes. Instead of what he terms "the magic of academic rituals of explanation," he chooses, he says, "to work with a different conflation of modernism and the primitivism it conjures into life— namely the carrying over into history of the principle of montage, as I learned that principle not only from terror, but from Putumayo shamanism with its adroit, albeit unconscious, use of the magic of history and its healing power."[51]

Taussig first uses his "principle of montage" to give us a close-up view of the role of terror which he sees as "the mediator par excellence of colonial hegemony."[52] In Taussig's treatment, terror is no simple reality; while it is certainly a mode of forcing labor from indigenous people, it is much more complex than that alone. Taussig hints that it is linked to the vary nature of human cultural being. "Behind the conscious self-interest that motivates terror and torture," Taussig writes, ". . . lie intricately construed, long-standing, unconscious cultural formations of meaning—modes of feeling—whose social network of tacit conventions and imagery lies in a symbolic world and not in that feeble 'pre-Kantian' fiction of the world represented by rationalism or utilitarian rationalism."[53]

While the geographic location of Taussig's description is the jungle of the South American rain forest, the symbolic location of terror that interests Taussig is the jungle of the civilized self. The wildness of the territory and the wildness of the Indians at home in it are matched, he claims, by the wildness hidden in the heart of the colonists and manifested in the ruthlessness of the terror they inflict. Taussig speaks of "the mimesis between the savagery attributed to the Indians by the colonists and the savagery perpetrated by the colonists in the name of . . . civilization, meaning business."[54] He asserts that "such mimesis occurs by a colonial mirroring of otherness that reflects back onto the colonists the barbarity of their own social relations, but as imputed to the savagery they yearn to colonize."[55]

This is very different hermeneutic territory from the liberalism of Ronald Wright cheering on indigenous resistance from the sidelines, or from the synthesizing scholarship of Lawrence Sullivan systematically domesticating exotic species of indigenous symbolic images. Taussig's description of the way in which projection of a savage otherness onto the indigenous peoples undergirds the practice of colonial terror for economic profit leads Western readers to ponder how complicit all interpretation may be in relation to indigenous peoples, to wonder at the hermeneutic complexity of hearing the authentic voice of the indigenous other, and to question whether Taussig himself has actually heard it, since his montage approach scarcely reveals a hermeneutic *modus operandi* that can be intelligibly grasped or replicated.

The centerpiece of Taussig's hermeneutic montage and its approach to indigenous otherness is shamanism. Taussig sees "wildness" as a quality which is projected onto indigenous persons so that they become "fetishized antiselves made by civilizing histories—the wildly contradictory figure of the Primitive, less than human and more than human."[56] Taussig claims that the desire of the colonists to appropriate to themselves the power of primitive reality led them to view the shamans as embodying the essential "wildness" of the indigenous other and to seek them out for healing precisely because they are "drenched in otherness."[57]

Shamanism figures as the central model for Taussig's critical contribution to hermeneutic theory which he terms "implicit social knowledge."[58] To understand the power of shamanism one must look, not to the shaman as such, but to the intersection of meanings and circumstances created by the "coming together of shaman and patient," and which "brings being and imagining together in a medley of swirling discourses—the shaman's song, the patient's narratives, the bawdiness, the leaden silences, the purging."[59] He rejects Claude Levi-Strauss' notion that "in their coming together, patient and shaman conduct on behalf of society a joint interrogation of their ideological environment."[60] Levi-Strauss' interpretation, claims Taussig, is "little more than a projection into magical ritual of the unstated ritual of academic explanation, turning chaos into order."[61] Taussig insists that:

> this magic of academe stands opposed, in its upright orderliness, to the type of sympathy necessary to understand that the healing song, magical or not, is but part of a baroque mosaic of discourses woven through stories, jokes, interjections, and hummings taking place not only through and on top of one another during the actual séance but before and after it as well.[62]

It is just such a "baroque mosaic of discourses" that Taussig aspires to create, or recreate, in the pages of his book.

Taussig lauds the disorder and chaos of the shamanic curing rites of ingesting hallucinogenic *yagé*, which has the power "to provoke sudden and infinite connections between dissimilars in an endless or almost endless process of connection-making and connection-breaking."[63] Taussig describes Putumayo shamans as resisting:

> the heroic mold into which current Western image-making would pour them. Instead their place is to bide time and exude bawdy vitality and good sharp sense by striking out in a chaotic zigzag fashion between laughter and death, constructing and breaking down a dramatic space layered out between these two poles.[64]

It is in such ritual contexts that Taussig locates his understanding of "implicit social knowledge," which he contrasts to normative Western models of knowledge. The shamanic experience is founded upon "the sensateness of human interrelatedness," whereas:

> the knowledge with which traditional Western philosophy from Plato to Kant is concerned cuts itself off from the type of sensory experience and power-riddled knowledge—implicit social knowledge—on which so much of human affairs and intellection rests. Sorcery and (so-called) shamanism, on the other hand, present modes of always locally built experience and image-formation in which such social knowledge is constitutive.[65]

This is an unusual hermeneutic turning of the tables in which a model for knowing is presented which takes its form from South American shamanism and is used to advance a critique of the fundamentals of Western epistemology.

Taussig's apparent hope for his hermeneutic of montage is to point the way to a newly authentic discourse. However, when he offers descriptions for this new discourse, such as "figuring the world through dialogue that comes alive with sudden transformative force in the crannies of everyday life's pauses and juxtapositions,"[66] it is not clear whether this represents a general method for comprehending the discourse of the other or if it is simply an *ex post facto* explanation of his own haphazard route to understanding. He is confident that anthropology in its ordinary self-conception "confounds itself in its very moment of understanding the natives' point of view,"[67] and he clearly intends to overcome that hermeneutic trap in his own interpretive approach. He insists that before there can be a sound anthropology in the context of a fully common discourse, "there has to be the long-awaited demythification and reenchantment of Western man in a quite different confluence of self and otherness."[68] Clearly, he understands his own work to be a contribution to that process.

The problematic crux of Taussig's book is not his effort toward the demythification of "Western man," but his potentially presumptive attempt to demythify indigenous reality. On one side, his work deserves praise since it is thoroughly grounded in personal experience with the social circumstances and ritual moments of indigenous life and serves as an antidote to romanticized versions of the other. On the other side of the crux, there lies the danger of the misappropriation of indigenous truth when a non-indigenous interpreter attempts to say truly what indigenous reality is. Taussig presents his interpretation as the antithesis of academic explanation, but it is also an explanation, and, however much it points to and is grounded in experience, it remains a highly intellectual explanation, one which is continually being connected throughout his book, either affirmatively or negatively, with leading figures in the Western intellectual firmament. Michael Taussig has, by way of a critical interpretation of South American shamanism, established his own quite specific position within the Western intelligentsia. Taussig seems to have projected onto Putumayo shamanism his montage theory, and its mirroring back to him a confirmative image comes as no great surprise.

Despite his sojourn among shamans and his participation in *yagé* curing rituals, in the end Taussig becomes only a more accomplished observer, the supreme subject both surveying and creating a whirling montage of indigenous signifiers. His own humanity disappears into his role as itinerant intellectual and there is no owning of his own being as a non-indigenous man, nor any reflection concerning his own investment in this immersion into and interpretation of indigenous life. In Taussig's montage, Putumayo shamanism is disempowered, since he presents its empowering as entirely a function of European projections on to it of primal otherness. Not believing there is any sacral dimension to this shamanism, Taussig interprets its meaning in thoroughly secular terms, that is, he demythologizes South American shamanism from a quite sophisticated, post-modern Europeanized world-view.

A COMMON FIELD OF DISCOURSE

Is there a way for us to move into a more authentic engagement with indigenous discourse than the hermeneutic sorties carried out by our three authors? Every sort of scholarly approach implies conventions of detachment which are inherently distancing and which covertly reinforce the normative character of the scholar's own cultural boundaries. If we are really to cross the borders constructed by our own discourse, two hermeneutic possibilities suggest themselves as moves beyond the previous efforts.

The first possibility is to follow Michael Taussig's lead in his pointing to ritual experience as a ground for discursive encounter. However, Taussig's penchant for reducing ritual meaning to social-psychological and political-economic signifiers prevented the otherness of indigenous ritual from being confronted in its sacral dimension. The very act of proposing ritual encounter as preparatory to discursive engagement raises the monotheist prohibition against entering any ritual space other than its own. It becomes immediately clear that the shamanic religions of the indigenous peoples of the "New World" have for 500 years marked a territory of otherness, a ritual space alien to and potentially dangerous for monotheistic Europeans. There can be no common field of discourse when there is no respect for the sacral values of the other, and not only lack of respect but often an active attribution of evil to the ritual reality of the indigenous other. An interpretive stance of this sort originates from a primal mode of fear which is not readily available to reflection. It is not otherness, but ones own fear, which is in need of demythologizing.

What is called for is a move into ritual encounter which perceives the otherness of indigenous ritual as an authentically human order of otherness and which respects the ontological Other as that which all human ritual seeks to encounter. A common field of discourse will only become possible when both stories grant human virtue to the rituals and religious world-views of the other, and a primary reason this has not occurred heretofore lies in the fear-bound need for presuming its own absoluteness on the part of monotheistic religion, notwithstanding that South American shamanism may have its own share of fear-bound issues.

The second hermeneutic possibility is to focus on the real flash point of otherness as it is perceived by the Europeans, which is what Taussig presumed to have accomplished. Again, however, Taussig misses the critical edge of otherness by pointing only to otherness which is projected by Europeans without examining the possibility that the heart of otherness is a sacral otherness. Authentic hermeneutic resolve would be to seek rapprochement precisely at the locus of the singular point of difference between indigenous ritual and European sensibilities. Presumably, this point will be the most significant danger spot, the most fearful symbol of the otherness of the other, and if one intends the transformation of understanding, then here is the logical place to take courage, risk the metamorphosis of your world-view, and invite knowledge of the other.

In sixteenth century Europe, the hands-down favorite for this role of the chief bugaboo of "New World" otherness was cannibalism. Anthony Pagden, in his book, *The Fall of Natural Man: The American Indian and the Origins of Comparative Ethnology*, remarks that "the European interest in man-eating amounts almost to an obsession,"[69] and that "by the end of the fifteenth century the anthropophagi had become a regular part of the topography of exotic lands."[70] Pagden notes that cannibalism was a key indicator as to whether a culture was to be categorized as civilized or as barbarian.[71] Michael Taussig similarly describes the white colonists in the late nineteenth century rain forest as being obsessed with cannibalism, but both Pagden and Taussig imply that cannibalism was something imputed to native peoples without substantive evidence of its actual practice.[72]

Why does cannibalism play this role as the distinguishing mark of otherness in European discourse, and what does it mean in indigenous discourse? Lawrence Sullivan helps flesh-out the indigenous view of cannibalism by describing the way South American mythologies recount how primordial beings produce transformations of the world order by their own dismemberment.[73] Sullivan notes that the Campa people consider the moon to be cannibalistic, and, at the same time, to be the author of life, provider of food, and inventor of the human birth process.[74] The moon, which is visibly dismembered and re-membered on a regular basis, may trigger a fundamental human recognition that cannibalism can be understood as related to the mystery of death and rebirth.

As for the European side of the matter, Anthony Pagden points out that the issue of what counted as food was of critical importance to fifteenth and sixteenth century Catholics. "Transubstantiation was a miracle which involved the transformation of one kind of food—a wafer—into another—the flesh of Christ himself."[75] The mystery of the Christian Eucharist is indeed a ritual devouring of an enfleshed divinity by whose death comes rebirth, and, therefore, it is symbolically related to ritual cannibalism.

European Judaism could be understood to belong to this comparison as well, since the central ritual of circumcision is a dismemberment rite which has ready analogues in indigenous ritual. Sullivan writes of South American mythology that, "body mutilation, especially through cutting, slicing, and tearing open, will take its meaning from incisive primordial events that fracture or dismember the primordium . . . to create new states of being."[76] Here, too, loss leads to generative power.

The hermeneutic effort to establish a common field of discourse cannot proceed successfully without confronting ritual otherness. When ritual otherness is confronted in the starkest mode of its otherness, namely, as cannibalism, what is discovered is not so much a case of terrible otherness as it is a case of uncomfortably close likeness. The genesis of the fear of otherness may lie in the fear of the resemblance of one ritual reality to the other.

The understanding of likeness projected as otherness can be facilitated by framing it within a history of religion which situates Near Eastern monotheism contextually as a participant in the patriarchal succession to the goddess-oriented, shamanic religion of Neolithic Eurasia by which the Bronze Age was inaugurated. Rituals of dismemberment may then be interpreted within a common re-membering of a more or less universal shamanic past, when death was the initiatory gateway to rebirth. Rediscovery of that sacral territory which human cultures mutually share can open the way to respectful listening, to the overcoming of fear, to the celebration of a common human way of being, and to the appreciation and enjoyment of one another's stories.

NOTES

1. Ronald Wright, *Stolen Continents. The Americas Through Indian Eyes Since 1942* (New York: Houghton Mifflin Co., 1992), 4.
2. Wright, 5.
3. Wright, 5.
4. See Wright, 5.
5. Wright, 7.
6. Wright, 10.
7. Wright, 4.

8. Wright, 8.

9. Wright, 8.

10. Wright, 9.

11. Cited by Wright, 16.

12. Wright, 16.

13. Wright, 14.

14. Wright, 149.

15. Wright, 150.

16. Wright, 150.

17. See Wright, 151-160.

18. Wright, 160.

19. Wright, 159.

20. Wright, 251.

21. Wright, 165.

22. Wright, 167.

23. Wright, 255.

24. Wright, 266.

25. Wright, 274.

26. Wright, 180.

27. See Wright, 181.

28. Wright, 276.

29. Wright, 278.

30. See Wright, 281.

31. See Wright, 279.

32. Lawrence E. Sullivan, *Icanchu's Drum: An Orientation to Meaning in South American Religions* (New York: Macmillan Pub. Co., 1988), 7.

33. Sullivan, 18.

34. Sullivan, 18.

35. Sullivan, 11.

36. Sullivan, 11.

37. See Sullivan, 26.

38. See Sullivan, 51.

39. See Sullivan, 73.

40. Sullivan, 48.

41. Sullivan, 78.

42. Sullivan, 79.

43. Sullivan, 107.

44. Sullivan, 107.

45. Sullivan, 20.

46. Sullivan, 31-32.

47. Sullivan, 9.

48. Michael Taussig, *Shamanism, Colonialism, and the Wild Man: A Study in Terror and Healing* (Chicago: University of Chicago Press, 1987), xviii.

49. Taussig, 24.

50. Taussig, xiii
51. Taussig, xiv.
52. Taussig, 5.
53. Taussig, 9.
54. Taussig, 134.
55. Taussig, 134.
56. Taussig, 240.
57. Taussig, 241.
58. Taussig, 366.
59. Taussig, 460.
60. Taussig, 460.
61. Taussig, 460.
62. Taussig, 460.
63. Taussig, 441.
64. Taussig, 444.
65. Taussig, 463.
66. Taussig, 209.
67. Taussig, 135.
68. Taussig, 135.
69. Anthony Pagden, *The Fall of Natural Man: The American Indian and the Origins of Comparative Ethnology* (Cambridge: Cambridge University Press, 1982), 80.
70. Pagden, 81.
71. Pagden, 80.
72. See Pagden, 82-83, and Taussig, 105.
73. See Sullivan, 79-87.
74. See Sullivan, 40.
75. Pagden, 88.
76. Sullivan, 86.

Catholic Evangelization in the Pueblo World

Gordon Bronitsky

INTRODUCTION

The first European to enter what is now New Mexico was Marcos de Niza, a Catholic priest who was a member of Don Juan de Oñate's pioneering exploration in 1539. New Mexico soon became one of the two major missionary frontiers in northwestern New Spain, the other being in Sonora. By 1700, all New Mexico Pueblo Indians were nominally Catholic. Nonetheless, the native religion has continued to flourish and true conversion was never attained. Instead, the Indians adopted a strategy of religious accommodation sometimes referred to as compartmentalization:

> . . . keeping their own organization and viewpoint quite separate from that of the Catholic Church, [the Pueblos] nevertheless accepted and sharply defined functions of the latter in their lives. They integrated fragments of Catholicism, but not the system, and hence it is no cause for wonder that the Catholic Church regarded no Pueblo village as a Catholic community.[1]

An understanding of the processes which gave rise to this phenomenon requires an examination of a variety of historical and cultural factors under Spanish, Mexican and then American rule. The first European to obtain information about the Pueblo peoples was Alvar Nuñez Cabeza de Vaca. He and three companions were shipwrecked on the Texas coast in 1528 and then proceeded to make their way on foot into northwestern New Spain. South of the present-day town of El Paso, Cabeza de Vaca learned of wealthy farming Indians in the upper Rio Grande who lived in large towns and who wove cotton blankets. In 1539, Fray Marcos de Niza, accompanied by Indian servants and a Negro, Esteban, who had been one of Cabeza de Vaca's party, traveled north to what are now the Zuñi villages in western New Mexico. Esteban entered the southernmost of these towns, Hawikuh, as advance for de Niza, and was killed by the Zuñi. Fray Marcos viewed the villages from a distance, claimed them for the king, and retreated back to New Spain.

On the basis of his exaggerated report, an expedition was outfitted in 1540 under Francisco Vásquez de Coronado for the conquest and conversion of the Pueblo peoples. Coronado's expedition included 300 soldiers and six Franciscan friars. The Pueblo country proved to be a disappointment, devoid of gold and treasure, despite explorations from western New Mexico to the Grand Canyon on the west and into the Great Plains on the east. The Spaniards established their headquarters during the winter of 1540-41 near Bernalillo; their levies of food and blankets on the neighboring Tiwa Pueblo Indians and the rape of several Indian women by Spanish soldiers led to resistance. Two Pueblos were burned to the ground and those inhabitants not sold into slavery were burned at the stake. As a result, the other Pueblos in the area abandoned their homes in mid-winter and the region was almost depopulated. In the spring of 1541, Coronado and his expedition returned to New Spain, leaving behind two Franciscan friars, who were martyred by the Indians.

No other formal expeditions visited the region until 1598, but several unauthorized parties made their way up the Rio Grande valley, exploring, looking for minerals and again, leaving behind Franciscan friars, who were again killed by the Indians. However, these expeditions did set the tone for Spanish-Indian relations which were to prevail until the 1650s. After initial peaceful contact with the Spaniards, oppression and misrule inevitably led to conflict. For example, the Espejo expedition in 1582 reported entering the Piro villages south of what is now Albuquerque:

> . . . the people came out to receive us, taking us to their pueblos and giving us a great quantity of turkeys, maize, beans, tortillas, and other kinds of bread.[2]

But the Spaniards came to explore and exploit the land and its people and could sustain themselves only by forcing tribute from the

Indians. When Indians revolted, they were put down with considerable brutality to enforce obedience and serve as an example to others.

Nonetheless, the Spanish subjugation of the Pueblo world differed significantly from the conquests of Cortes among the Aztecs or Pizarro in Peru. There was no overthrow of native states; in fact, by the time of Oñate's colonization of New Mexico in 1598, the word "conquest" had been legally banished.

THE SPANISH PERIOD

What was the background to Spanish settlement in the Pueblo world? Under pressure from church and legal authorities, Philip II had set forth the Royal Ordinance of 1573.[3] This imposed considerable restriction on Spanish settlement and treatment of the Indians. Most notably, settlers were forbidden to engage in "conquest" and were instead required to pacify the native people by resort to nonviolent means. However, the differences between theory and practice in the Pueblo world were considerable.

Formal colonization of New Mexico began in 1598 with the expedition of Juan de Oñate, a group of 400 soldiers, colonists, friars, and Mexican Indian servants. The motive for expansion was primarily religious, the goal being to Christianize one of the last large populations of sedentary agricultural Indians in New Spain. On July 7, 1598, Oñate met at Santo Domingo Pueblo with leaders of several Pueblo villages, lectured them on Spanish politics and religion, and then received their declaration of allegiance to the Spanish crown. On September 8, New Mexico was declared a missionary province of the Franciscan order and the pueblos were allotted to individual friars.

Ultimately, Oñate failed to find mineral wealth and was removed from the governorship of the province in 1607. In 1609, the capital was formally established at Santa Fe, and the missionization of New Mexico began in earnest. Major sources of information about this mission period are the memorials of Fray Alonso de Benavides, who became *custos,* or chief prelate, of the New Mexican missions.[4]

The Pueblo of Santo Domingo was chosen as ecclesiastical capital and churches were built with Indian labor at Pecos, Acoma, the Hopi village of Awatovi, at sites among the Tompiros, Southern Tiwa, Jemez, and elsewhere. Due to lack of sufficient missionary personnel, chapels, known as *visitas,* were placed in smaller towns and served by clergy from the nearest mission center, where one or more friars maintained residence. With the baptism of the people and the building of a church or chapel, each Pueblo became a *doctrina* or Indian parish. The missionaries selected Indian lay assistants, known as *fiscales de doctrinas*, to serve as teacher and interpreters, and native *alguaciles* to enforce religious discipline.

The economic changes designed by the Spaniards to integrate the people into provincial society were an integral part of the mission program. Missions maintained schools and shops, which taught mechanical arts as well as religion. Native smiths made and repaired iron tools, and mission schools taught improved farming techniques and introduced new crops and animal husbandry as well.

These Spanish missions served to some degree as shields against the demands of the civil government, and conflict between civil and church authorities over Indian lands and labor characterized much of the seventeenth century. Nonetheless, the missions aroused considerable hostility among the Pueblo peoples, first for their strict demands and discipline for infraction of church rules, and second for their war on what they considered the idolatry of the Pueblos. Masked kachina dances were prohibited and periodic raids upon places of worship resulted in confiscation and public burning of sacred paraphernalia. As a result, the native priesthood and the Spaniards became implacable enemies, and much of the native religion went underground. A veneer of Spanish Catholicism was imposed over the Pueblo religion and values, which continued to flourish.

A major concern of the Spaniards was the legal justification for their acts. Much more than other European powers, Spain was acutely concerned with the legal and moral treatment of Indians. The church, for instance, upheld equality of Indians and argued for their admission as equals into colonial society once they passed from neophytes to full membership in the church. The civil authorities, in accepting the native people as their vassals, agreed with the same principle. However, the conquistador-colonial class could only regard such rules as hostile to its own fortunes, since maintenance of permanent political dominance and social privilege depended on keeping Indians in the subservient role that implied natural inequality.

This conflict of motives led to open rivalry between the clergy and civil authorities and provoked struggles for supremacy. The kings, attempting to reconcile differences and protect Indians, passed endless legislation that was generally ignored.

This civil strife hindered attempts to fully convert the Indians. The Franciscans emphasized a long civilizing process of missionization in which simplified methods of indoctrination stressed veneration of the Cross, respect for the clergy, instruction in the sacraments, teaching of elementary prayers, and regular attendance at religious services.[5]

Tensions were further exacerbated because the crown was committed to the expenditure of large sums on the missions and an ample Indian population was available as a labor force. As a result, New Mexican friars often built churches and convents far larger than required. In addition, Pueblo lands were designated for support of the clergy, but these usually exceeded the actual physical needs of the priests, thus allowing them to convert surpluses to their own profit. The result was the development of strong vested interests among missionaries, whose preservation depended upon retention of the Indians in a state of tutelage.

Civil authorities also made demands upon Indian land labor under the *encomienda*, which added to the burdens on the already strained Indian economy. Under the *encomienda*, individuals (the *encomenderos*), were entitled to collect annual tribute from a specified town or group of Indians. The *encomendero* was expected to act as a trustee over his tributary subjects, providing material aid to their church and offering military protection. Tribute demands, although restricted in legal theory, were often abused.

An even greater burden on Indian communities was the *repartimiento,* a system of forced labor which provided workers for Spanish farms and haciendas, usually without pay. In the first half of the seventeenth century, the ratio of Spaniard to Indian was such that the number of workers was greater than the labor demands of the settlers. However, after 1665, famine, pestilence and raids by nomadic Indians so reduced the Pueblo people that it became almost impossible to meet these demands.[6]

Spanish demands for labor, the rape of Pueblo women, famine and epidemic, all contributed to Pueblo unrest. As early as 1632, the Zuñi revolted and murdered their priest. Sporadic rebellions occurred throughout the seventeenth century, often sparked by Spanish suppression of the native religion. In 1655, a delegation of Hopi came to Santa Fe to denounce their priest who had whipped an Indian for practicing idolatry, then doused him with turpentine and set him afire.[7]

Spanish control was further weakened by rivalry between the civil authorities and the Franciscans over control of the Pueblo people. Both sides accused each other of exploiting the Indians; both sides encouraged the Indians to resist the demands of the other.

The situation exploded on August 10, 1680 with the Pueblo Revolt. Led by Popé, the governor of San Juan Pueblo, who had been whipped for idolatry in 1675, the Pueblos formed an alliance and rose up in revolt. Twenty-one missionaries and 400 colonists were killed immediately. Many of the surviving colonists fled for safety to Santa Fe, which was besieged for nine days by Pueblo troops. The survivors then fled to the safety of El Paso under Governor Otermin, leaving the haciendas, towns, and ranches of New Mexico in flaming ruins.[8]

However, the Revolt also weakened the Pueblos because of battle deaths, starvation, and enslavement. Raids by neighboring nomadic tribes sharply increased. By the 1693 Spanish reconquest, the number of inhabited villages had dropped sharply and many villages had been relocated. The Spanish reconquest, in turn, led to further population decline and dislocation; the Tano Pueblos south of Santa Fe fled to the security of the Hopi mesas in northeastern Arizona, which were never conquered by the Spaniards, and remained there. The Hopi village of Awatovi permitted Franciscans to resume mission work; the other Hopi, furious at this concession, massacred its inhabitants.[9]

By 1700, the Spaniards were again firmly in control of the Pueblo world, with the exception of the Hopi, but the situation had changed. The Spaniards learned from experience and abolished the *encomienda* system. The missionary system, although reintroduced, never regained its authority, in part due to a marked decline in the number of Franciscans and in part due to significant reduction in Indian population. Spaniards soon outnumbered Indians in New Mexico. The large haciendas, with their demand for Indian labor, were largely replaced by the growth of small farms, which relied on their own members for labor. The civil authorities became much more responsive to Indian complaints of maltreatment, due in large part to the growing menace of raids from nomadic Indians who threatened Spaniard and Pueblo alike. Pueblo Indians served regularly as valued allies of the Spanish army, and Pueblo communities began to flourish, raising agricultural and wool products for the regional economy.

By 1800, the Pueblo Indians were a secure part of New Mexican society, largely left alone by the Franciscans as long as they conformed superficially to outward practices of Christianity. By late 1820, most of the Pueblos had taken advantage of official proclamations to establish formal municipal governments, obtaining full citizenship and legal equality.

THE MEXICAN PERIOD, 1821-1846

Although the Mexican period saw some significant changes in relations between local authorities and nomadic Indians and a major decline in protection of Indian land and water rights, Pueblo religion was little affected. By 1832, there were only five missionaries among all the New Mexican Pueblos, and their efforts were largely ineffectual. In 1833, Bishop José Antonio de Zubiría of Durango, whose jurisdiction included New Mexico, made an official visit and deplored the state of the missionary program, noting that mission structures were in disrepair, vessels and vestments worn out, and that many Pueblos had returned to idolatry.[10] Rather than a return to idolatry, however, the Pueblos were simply practicing more openly rituals which had continued throughout the Spanish period. Once again, ceremonies were given in the plazas, open to observation by non-Indians, indicating that the native religion continued to be strong and vital.

THE AMERICAN PERIOD

The Pueblo world underwent considerable changes in the American period as Pueblo communities lost political power and absorbed elements of expanding Anglo-American culture. As Anglo-American influence became more pervasive, Pueblos began to emphasize the boundaries of their traditional lifestyle in order to stave off total erosion. As part of this process, many Spanish elements not only persisted but came to be identified as part of the Pueblo cultural framework.

A key element in this process was the Catholic Church. The Church came to play a major role in defending Pueblo communities against the aggressive inroads of Protestant missionaries. Indeed, in several villages, Pueblo leaders denounced those of their communities who converted to Protestantism as traitors to the Indian way.[11]

In 1850, the Bishop of Durango made what was to be the final inspection of the Upper Rio Grande churches and missions from his bishopric. He found a ministry in considerable decline. Soon afterward, the New Mexico Territory was elevated to episcopal rank and in 1851, French-born John Lamy became New Mexico's first resident bishop. Lamy was appalled by the lack of discipline among clergy and laity and instituted a controversial policy of reform. Some priests quit and were replaced by priests recruited in France. Lamy devoted most of his efforts to reviving Catholicism among the Hispanic population, largely neglecting the Pueblos. Lack of funds and remoteness hampered the few priests still working in Indian villages. As late as the end of the century, the Catholic Church counted a Catholic Pueblo population of some 18,000, but maintained only two day schools and two boarding schools.[12]

Protestants saw the Pueblo world as a fertile field for missionization and began entering the Southwest soon after the American occupation commenced in 1846. Although mission schools were established, the Protestants made almost no converts through 1870. Political corruption in the Indian Bureau led to the establishment of a new federal policy in 1869 in which religious denominations were encouraged to found schools on reservations, but not until the 1890s did Protestant denominations enter the Pueblo world to a major degree. Protestants continued to meet with marked lack of success for many reasons, most notably their condemnation of all Pueblo religious practices and their demand that converts sever themselves from Pueblo society. Pueblo resistance to these demands was supported by the Catholic Church which by now viewed Pueblo religious rituals as an integral part of Pueblo Catholicism. Pueblo converts to Protestantism usually left the community, further strengthening the traditional religious leaders and the Catholic Church.

The standoff between traditional religion and Catholicism continues today. In the 1950s, conflicts between the Pueblo community of Isleta and their priest over traditional religious ceremonies led to the priest being escorted off the reservation in handcuffs by tribal leaders, followed by a court order which continues to prohibit the priest from entering the Pueblo.[13] Nonetheless, the Pueblo of Isleta is also proud of the fact that the first Pueblo Indian ordained as a Catholic priest is from Isleta. However, the fact that this ordination occurred in 1977, 438 years after the entrance of the first Catholic priests, and 379 years after the institution of a regular program of missionization, is also a testament to the enduring strength of the native religion. As one Pueblo woman once explained to me, "On the outside, we are Catholics, but our [native] religion is in our hearts."

NOTES

1. Edward Spicer, *Cycles of Conquest: The Impact of Spain, Mexico and the United States on the Indians of the Southwest, 1533-1960* (Tucson: University of Arizona Press, 1962), 508.

2. Harold E. Bolton, ed., *Spanish Exploration in the Southwest, 1542-1706* (New York: Charles Scribners Sons, 1916), 177.

3. Juan F. Pacheco, and Francisco de Cárdenas y Espejo, *Colección de Documentos Inéditos, Relativos al Descubrimiento, Conquista y Organización de las Antiguas Posesiones Españolas de América y Oceania,* 42 vols. (Madrid: M.B. de Quirós, 1864-1884).

4. Alonso Benavides, *Fray Alonso de Benavides' Revised Memorial of 1634,* ed. F. Hodge, G. Hammond, and A. Rey (Albuquerque: University of New Mexico Press, 1945).

5. Francis Scholes, "Church and State in New Mexico, 1610-1650," *New Mexico Historical Review* 11 no. 1 (1936): 9-76; no. 2: 145-178; no. 3: 283-294; no. 4: 297-349; 12 no. 1 (1937): 78-106.

6. Marc Simmons, "History of Pueblo-Spanish Relations to 1821,) *Handbook of North American Indians,* vol. 9: *Southwest,* ed. A. Ortiz. (Washington, DC: Smithsonian Institution, 1979), 183.

7. Simmons, 184.

8. Charles Hackett, ed., *Revolt of the Pueblo Indians of New Mexico and Otermin's Attempted Reconquest* (Albuquerque: University of New Mexico Press, 1942).

9. Simmons, 187.

10. Lansing Bloom, "New Mexico Under Mexican Administration, 1821-1846," *Old Santa Fe Genealogy and Biography* 1 no. 1 (1913-1914): 3-49.

11. Simmons, 208.

12. Simmons, 213.

13. John Olguin and Michael Olguin, "Isleta—The Pueblo That Roared," *Indian Historian* 9 no. 4 (1976): 2-13.

American Indians, Ten Lost Tribes and Christian Eschatology

Gershon Greenberg

There is of course no scientific evidence to the Ten Lost Tribes-American Indian connection, only evidence to the contrary. But the belief in the connection was a serious religious, and mythic, concern. Among those religions in America which enunciated the belief that American Indians were descendants of the Ten Lost Tribes[1]—and this includes early Catholics, the Mormons and at least one Jew, Mordecai Manuel Noah[2]—the Protestants of millennialist orientation were the most deeply involved.

I will begin with John Eliot's (1780-1803) work in 1651, continue through Charles Crawford (1752-1815), Elias Boudinot (1740-1821) and Ethan Smith (1786-1849), and end with Barbara A. Simon (writing 1823-1836). For these millennialist Protestants, the identification of American Indians as descendants of the Ten Lost Tribes was bound up with Christian eschatology.[3] The authors shared a commitment to America as the place where descendants of the people of ancient Hebrew Scripture lived, and where they would convert to Christianity at the eve of or during the apocalypse.

JOHN ELIOT

Eliot, trained at Cambridge University, was converted under the influence of Puritan leader Thomas Hooker (1586-1647): "[T]he Lord said to my dead soul, *live*. And through the grace of Christ, I do live, and I shall live forever!"[4] Eliot came to New England in 1631, where he would become known as the "apostle of the Indians."

Eliot envisioned world history as a cosmic war between the forces of Christ and the forces of evil and believed that history was reaching the point—he did not offer dates—when Christ would victor over evil in the form of Antichrist the Roman Catholic Church. Then Christ would reign over the earth; all peoples of the world—church and government together—would be ruled by the word of God.[5] Christ's reign included the conversion of the Jews: "[Y]ou shall see the mighty power of gospel grace of Christ Jesus, in the conversion both of Jews and gentiles, and so going on until the last and final conversion of the Jews, which we hope for at this day. . . . Christ hath opened heaven for all that will come unto Him, gentiles as well as Jews."[6]

In 1649 and 1660 Eliot described the role of American Indians in this eschatology, as descendants of the Israelites. The Ten Lost Tribes-American Indian connection was accepted in Puritan circles, notably by Englishmen John Dury and Thomas Thorowgood.[7] Eliot himself believed that Hebrew entry into America originated in the days of Shem's great-great grandson Ever's son Peleg, when the earth divided and Peleg's descendants ended up in the "eastern world" ("east" here, because of the route taken) (Genesis 10:22-25). The second immigration began in 722 BCE when the kingdom of Israel fell and the ten tribes of the northern kingdoms were exiled into Assyria (II Kings 17:6). Drawing a linguistic connection, Eliot observed that the ten Hebrew (*Ivri*) tribes went to "lands beyond (*me'ever*) the rivers" (Isaiah 18:1-2), to the easternmost limits of the world, namely America.[8] There they met up with their predecessors, with whom they had a "common language." Eliot explained that the Ten Lost Tribes suffered less than their brethren, the descendants of Judah and Benjamin, who were responsible for the crucifixion (Ezekiel 16:46).

Eliot first thought the Jews of the world would have to convert before the Ten Lost Tribes ("Because til the Jews come in, there is a seal set upon the hearts of those [Indian] people, as they think from some apocalyptical places"),[9] but changed his mind. At the *eschaton* the Ten Lost Tribes would be the first of Israel to receive God's grace, become Christian and return to the Land of Israel to share in Christ's kingdom. At the end of history God would "gather the scattered and lost dust of our bodies. At the resurrection [He] will find out these lost and scattered Israelites, and in finding them, bring in with them the [gentile] nations among whom they were scattered (*e.g.,* Romans 11:17), and so shall Jacob's promise extend to a multitude of nations." Indeed, God's glory at the *eschaton* would be manifest first in the east: In Ezekiel's vision the Temple's eastern gate was measured first (Ezekiel

40:6), God's glory entered the Temple through it (Ezekiel 43:1-3), and the sanctuary's precious waters issued eastward (Ezekiel 47:1). From there, America, it would proceed to the western world, namely Europe: "God grant that the old bottles of the western world be not so incapable of the new wine of Christ [and] His expected kingdom; that the eastern bottles be not the only [containers] thereof for a season."[10]

For Eliot, then, the Ten Lost Tribes-American Indian tie, the conversion and apocalypse, reinforced one another. If history was reaching its end, as he believed, the lost Israelites would have to be found; once found, they would have to be converted in preparation of the establishment of Christ's Jerusalem-centered kingdom and their return thereto. Eliot committed his own life to help effectuate the process.

CHARLES CRAWFORD

Born in Antigua, Crawford attended Cambridge University and arrived in America ca. 1782. He wrote poetry and philosophical studies,[11] but his major interest was Christian eschatology. In this latter context he explored the Ten Lost Tribes origin of the American Indians. While Eliot used Scripture and Puritan views to define his position, Crawford drew upon the first hand reports of Pierre Charlevoix (1761)[12] and William Bartram (1791)[13] for data about Indians in general and from Thorowgood, William Penn (1683),[14] Jonathan Edwards (1758),[15] Charles Beatty (1768)[16] and, most importantly, James Adair (1775) for information about the Ten Lost Tribe-Indian connection. James Adair drew these similarities:

1. Indian society was structured according to tribal divisions defined by linear descent. Each tribe had its special symbol which, like the biblical cherubim (Ezekiel 10:14-15), was an animal.
2. The Indians regarded their deity as the direct head of state.
3. The Indians regarded themselves as unique and chosen from among the rest of mankind. They were the "beloved" and "holy" people, while whites were contemptible and "accursed people." God was ever-present to them and offered direction through prophets, while the whites were alienated, outlaws to the Indian covenant with God. The conviction of chosenness

"alike animates both the white Jew and the red American with that steady hatred against all the world except themselves."

4. Indians divided the year into spring, summer, autumn and winter, and they began the year with the first new moon of the vernal equinox. Like the Israelites before 70 C.E., the Indians designated months with numbers. The Israelites called the seventh month *Aviv* (Exodus 9:31, Deuteronomy 16:1), which also meant unripened corn; and the Indians had a Passover-like celebration known as the "green corn dance."

5. The Indians had prophets and priests and a *sanctum sanctorum* (holy of holies) housing consecrated vessels, which the laity could not approach. The priestly order, called "Ishtoallo" (a corruption of "*Ish Ha'elohim*," II Kings 4:16ff), possessed a divine spirit enabling its members to foretell the future and control the course of nature. The spirit was transmitted to their children, who kept related sacred laws. When the high priest made a holy fire for the yearly atonement ceremony, he wore a white ephod (a sleeveless waistcoat) and breastplate of white conch shell with two bored holes for attaching buckhorn buttons fastened to straps of skin (Exodus 28).

6. The Indian god was a great supreme holy spirit, the "Great Yohewah" who dwelt above the clouds but also with the good people. No tribe attempted to form an image of this god. The Indians had a mysterious name for the Great Spirit which, like the Israelite tetragrammaton, was not to be employed in common speech. When they used it to invoke God in solemn hymns, they spent a full breath on each of the two first syllables of the awesome divine name.

7. According to Indian tradition, their forefathers came from a distant country in remote ages and moved eastward until they settled east of the Mississippi. How did they cross the water between the continents? According to Plato's *Timaeus*, the land of Atlantis was originally torn asunder from the eastern continent. Atlantis was America, and the crossing was made over islands in the narrow strait between northeast Asia and northwest America.

8. The Indians had a practice according to which the surviving brother of a man who died childless was to marry the widow and raise seed for his brother. A widow was bound to mourn the death of her husband for at least three years, unless the brother of the deceased husband wished to take her. In that

case she was released from the law as soon as the brother made love to her.

9. The Indians had a sacred ark of the covenant, which they never placed directly on the ground but rather rested on stones or logs. They carried it when they went into battle. Only the chieftain could handle it, and it was deemed dangerous even for sanctified warriors to touch it.

10. The Indians obliged women in their "lunar retreats" to separate themselves, and remain at a distance at the risk of their lives. "It conveys a most horrid and dangerous pollution to those who touch, or go near them, or walk anywhere within the circle of their retreats; and are in fear of spoiling the supposed purity and power of their holy ark."[17]

In Crawford's view the downfall of Antichrist (e.g., Daniel's "little horn," Daniel 7:8) in the form of Roman Catholicism—Rome was Revelation's "drunken with blood" (Revelation 17:6)—and Islam was imminent. The end of Rome would include the collapse of religious orders (especially Jesuits), the "second beast" who enlivened the "first beast," Rome (Revelation 13:11-12). To Crawford, Islam meant the Turkish empire, citing Daniel's vision of the destruction of those who indulged in unnatural lusts (Daniel 11). Following the abolition of the papacy, true Christians would join together to expel the Turks from the Holy Land (Luke 21:24). Crawford calculated the downfall for ca. 2000 by joining Daniel's "dividing of time" with John's 42 months (Daniel 8:25, Revelation 13:5), deducing 1260 years (42 months x 30 days). As to when the 1260 years began, he cited the alternatives of the reign of Pope Gregory I (590-604), Roman Emperor Phocas' concession to the Pope (in 607, Phocas granted Boniface III's request for the See's privileged position in the hierarchy), and the Pope's assertion of temporal monarchy with the destruction of the Exarchate of Ravenna (The conquering Franks gave Ravenna to the popes in 754).[18]

What would happen to the Jews during the apocalypse? Crawford was not against Jews per se; but he did expect them to become Christian at the eschaton. Thus in 1803 he spoke of the dispersion of the Jews without their destruction as fulfilling God-inspired prophecy (Deuteronomy 28:64).[19] In 1817 he referred to Isaiah's statements about the one who was oppressed and slaughtered—without reference to Jewish responsibility for the crucifixion:

[These passages in chapter 53] apply explicitly to Jesus Christ. He suffered silently the injustice of the oppressor. He was taken from prison and led to the cross. 'Christ (says Tacitus) was punished by Pontius Pilate under the Tiberius regime.' He suffered not for His own guilt, but for the trespass of others.[20]

Crawford, indeed, appealed to German Emperor Joseph for the "unlimited toleration" of Jews. The appeal was connected, however, to "concomitant events" relating to the apocalyptic fall of the Antichrist. Specifically, the Jews would return:

It is said in Scripture that when the race of Israel shall return unto the Lord their God, that then He will gather them from all the nations whither they have been scattered, into the Land which their fathers possessed, and will put on their enemies and those who persecute them, the curses which they themselves have known [Deuteronomy 30].

The Christian saints of God would "receive the dominion [including the Holy Land] of the [Turkish] beast" (Daniel 7:26-27) and the Jews would convert. If not, Crawford held out the possibility of Christian war against them. Jesus' servants did not fight to deliver Him from the Jews, he explained, because His kingdom was not of this world [John 18:35-36]. But with the apocalypse the world would become Christ's kingdom, and His servants could fight.[21] Crawford anticipated that the Jews would return to the "Land of their forefathers in the latter part of the next century, before the year 1900." Referring again to the 1260 years, he identified their start, as far as the Jews were concerned, with either 614 when Jerusalem was taken by the Persians or 622 when the Hegira took place.[22]

What of the Ten Lost Tribes-American Indian tie? Crawford also referred to the split of the globe in Peleg's days, when Noah's descendants ended up in the land divided off from Asia—namely America. They were joined, sometime after 722 BCE, by the Ten Lost Tribes. Crawford reiterated the similarities published by Adair *et al*— *e.g.* female purity and isolation during menstrual cycles; belief in one God, in the human soul and its immortality; the tradition of a great deluge. He also added some of his own. He thought that scalping was recorded in Psalms [Psalms 68:2], and related how "a person of information, whose appointments led him to be frequently in the country of the Indians" told him that some Indians had the custom, "in imitation of the Jews, to carry the amputated part [of the enemy's body, *i.e.*, castration] in triumph," following David's practice with the Philistines (I Samuel 18:27). Crawford also cited a "learned Jew," "son of a Jewish rabbi or a rabbi himself," a convert to Christianity, who testified about the Ten Lost Tribes connection. This convert left Great Britain for Philadelphia before 1787. Believing that many American Indians were descendants of the ten tribes, he went to live among them (probably the Chickasaws) "to learn their language, that he might teach them the gospel and proceed with them in person to Jerusalem." After a short time among them, however, he died—of natural causes.

Crawford hoped for a missionary to explain to the Indians how their ancestors were God's favorite people who were delivered from Egypt; how their God descended upon Mt. Sinai to give the ten commandments; about the messianic prophecies. Once they learned their heritage, Crawford was sure, they would convert. Crawford believed the Indian conversion would occur "before a very great length of time." He decided that when the Jews from around the world would gather (*ca* 1900), so would the Indian converts, passing over the Bering Straits in tribes into Asia (Isaiah 43:5-6). It was a "sure word of prophecy [II Peter 1:19] . . . that all the descendants of the House of Israel, among which are many Indians, will be restored to the Land of their forefathers. The time is not far distant when this restoration will be effected." In an intriguing (and self-serving) coincidence, Crawford predicted that "Many of the Indians will then relinquish their land to the white people."[23]

Thus for Crawford, as for Eliot, the Ten Lost Tribes-American Indian tie was tied to Christian eschatology. He anticipated restoration and conversion of the Jews, including American Indians (around 1900), as a prelude to the fall of Antichrist (around 2000). Contemporary missionary work was part of the process leading up to the apocalypse and final reign of Christ on earth. Specifically, the Indians' knowledge of their Israelite identity enabled their conversion; and conversion enhanced the process of ingathering which was a sign of the *eschaton*. Of course, the ingathering and subsequent kingdom of Christ would not be possible unless the Ten Lost Tribes were first discovered by Christians. There was considerable pressure on those who expected the fall of Antichrist, such as Crawford himself, to make (or "create") the discovery; the work in history had to be aligned with the cosmic events unfolding from above.

ELIAS BOUDINOT

The distinguished Elias Boudinot, a French Hougenot, was president of the Continental Congress, founding president of the American Bible Society, a member of the American Board of Commissioners of Foreign Missions, and author of works in the Christian religion.[24] Boudinot shared the formula of his predecessors: He believed in the truths of the book of Revelation and the fall of the antichrist as Rome in particular. The *eschaton* was imminent, Jews would convert and be restored to their Land, and American Indians as descendants of the Ten Lost Tribes would be included. Boudinot added a special role for America.

Unlike Crawford, Boudinot dwelled on Israel's deficiencies. At the time of Jesus, Jews were misled into thinking that the messiah would deliver them from the temporal yoke of Rome:

> [T]he Jews, forsaking the natural and plain sense of the language of their prophets, and wholly mistaking the nature of the true church or kingdom of the Messiah . . . could not feel the power of Christ's arguments. . . . Thus blinded and misled by their strong ideas of the kingdom of the Messiah being of this world, and specially designed by God to deliver them from the Roman yoke, as well as from all other temporal enemies . . . they had no settled ideas of the nature of that life and immortality which were so clearly brought to light by the gospel. This paved the way for their temporary rejection and dispersion, in fulfillment of the very prophecies on which they founded their peculiar tenets relative to the temporal kingdom of their expected Messiah.

The destruction of the Temple of Jerusalem was a consequence to Jewish disbelief and an affirmation of Christian faith (Hebrews 10, Revelation 11:12, Luke 21). The dispersion of the Jews, their affliction, their being reviled, were all "a conspicuous monument" of the truth of Daniel's prophecy:

> Thus the first coming of Christ was ascertained clearly, so as to be sufficient for the conviction of the most obstinate. . . . [The] important events that were to happen during [Daniel's] period of 70 weeks or 490 years were ascertained [in advance], *i.e.,* the coming of the Messiah—His crucifixion—and the destruction of the Temple and city of Jerusalem [Daniel 10:25].

Boudinot observed, however, that those who persecuted the Jews were degenerate—they did not knowingly act on God's behalf—and would be punished; their "time" would come [Luke 21].

At the end of history, however, all Jews living and dead would be restored and converted. The veil blocking the vision of Christ's second coming would be removed—a veil which until Boudinot's day "the readers in the Jewish worship have hanging over their faces [until today] while they read the law of Moses to the congregation." At His second advent the church would be "completed," and once this took place "the race existing at our Lord's appearance in the flesh [which] so completely lost sight of [the promise of resurrection]" would be resurrected. Complete Israel, now Christian, would inherit the Land (Acts 7:5, Hebrews 11:19).[25]

Boudinot, citing a variety of scriptural sources (*e.g.* Jeremiah 3:8, Amos 8:9, II Esdras 13:41), pointed out that while the descendants of the tribes of Judah and Benjamin "perversely put [the Messiah] to death on the cross, and voluntarily imprecated that His blood might rest on them and their children" (Matthew 27:25), the remaining ten, who were innocent of this crime, ended up in America. Following Eliot, Boudinot observed that because they were not involved in the crucifixion, the ten suffered less. He spoke of the American Indians as "subjects of God's protection and gracious care," and "children of God's watchful providence."[26] Subsequent to Christ's initial advent, all would be located and restored. Citing Edward King (1795-1837), who had committed his own life to proving the Ten Lost Tribes-American Indian tie,[27] Boudinot stated that after Christ's arrival there would be "a very long period of time ... during which all things shall be restored, and every soul of every kind shall be placed in its proper lot and station according to that divine promise made to Daniel" (Daniel 12:13).[28] In particular, the American Indians would be discovered, converted to Christianity and aided in returning to Jerusalem and the Land of Israel.[29] Following Crawford, Boudinot wanted the Indians to be told of their legacy, of which they had become ignorant. "The Indians have so degenerated, that they cannot at this time give any tolerable account of the origin of their religious rites, ceremonies and histories."[30]

The fact that Christ's advent involved the Ten Lost Tribes, led Boudinot to speculate that the United States existed in order to preserve the Ten Lost Tribes' descendants intact until Christ came: "Who knows, but God has raised up these United States in these latter days for the very purpose of accomplishing His will in bringing His beloved people to their own Land?"[31] Furthermore, following Eliot, Boudinot was convinced that Christ would act first in America:

> Jehovah will call from the East the eagle. And from a far distant land [will call] the man of counsel [Isaiah 46:11], to bring to pass the design He has formed, and He shall execute it. For the Messiah shall raise up the scions of Jacob and restore the breaches of Israel.

> [If] the northwest parts of America are near the northeast parts of Asia, near Kamchatka, as the late discoveries seem to give reason to believe; and if the lost tribes of Israel passed over this strait to America and are to be found there, as Messrs. [John] Eliot, [William] Penn and others have supposed, then it is possible that the eagle and the man of his counsel may come from that far distant land, and by passing over the same strait to the northeast part of Asia, may be said to come from the east.[32]

Thus, Boudinot shared his predecessors' tripartite apocalyptic *Weltanschauung:* Christ's kingdom, return-conversion of known Jews, and the discovery-conversion-return of the American Indians. The descendants of the Ten Lost Tribes enjoyed a special place in history and eschatology. They were not responsible for the crucifixion as were Judah and Benjamin, and so did not bear the consequences of dispersion and suffering. They resided in America under God's care, and would continue to do so until Christ's arrival. Boudinot's America was not only the scene of the onset of the advent: its ultimate role in history was to preserve the Ten Lost Tribes until the advent began.

ETHAN SMITH

Smith was a Congregational pastor in Hopkinton, New Hampshire; Poultney, Vermont; and Hanover, Massachusetts. According to David Persuitte, he was the source for Joseph Smith's statements in the Book of Mormon on the Ten Lost Tribes and Jews.[33] In addition to Beatty, Adair and Bartram, Smith drew upon a variety of first hand reports, notably those of renowned geographer and Congregationalist leader Jedidiah Morse (1761-1826).[34]

For Smith too the Christian *eschaton* ("millennial kingdom of Christ") was imminent. He thought that the (unidentified) "signs of the times" (*e.g.*, Matthew 16:3) had been in place for some thirty years. Like his predecessors he identified the destruction of Antichrist ("the battle of that great day of God Almighty") with that of Rome. Like Boudinot ("This fall of the mystical Babylon [Rome] is to answer the same purpose to the Christian world, that the desolation of the Jewish state and the Temple did to the believing Jews, soon after our Savior's resurrection"),[35] Smith spoke of Jerusalem's destruction forty years after Christ's ascension as prefiguring the end to Rome.

As to the Jews: The descendants of Judah and Benjamin crucified Christ and fell under the full execution of His wrath. Moses already told them that God would cut them off for their transgressions, "and the Messiah uttered against them, in consequence of their rejecting Him, a new edition of these fatal denunciations" (Matthew 24, Luke 19, 21, 23).[36] At the end of history the Jews traceable to Judah and Benjamin would undergo conversion and return. In fact, Smith considered the process well underway. The Jews in Poland, for example, "seem to be convinced that some important change in their condition is preparing; and they seem ready to cooperate in the means of such a change." He cited the efforts of the American Society for Meliorating the Condition of the Jews (founded in 1816 as the American Society for Evangelizing Jews) and Joseph Wolff's mission in Palestine and "the remarkable conversion [there] of many of the Jews."

What of the Ten Lost Tribes? Drawing from Charlevoix, Beatty, Adair and Boudinot, as well as a variety of other sources such as Samuel Jarvis (1786-1851),[37] Smith pointed to such similarities as the Long Island Indian belief in one supreme God, Creek refuge cities, Chipewyan tradition of a great deluge, Sioux belief in man's creation by God from the earth's dust and the reverence for one tribe, namely the Mohawks. These "savage" and "outcast" people (Isaiah 11:12) were now to be restored. Isaiah's voice crying in the wilderness to prepare the way of God (Isaiah 40:3) applied to them:

> The voice, which restores Israel, is heard in the *vast wilderness of America*, a literal wilderness of thousands of miles, where the dry bones of the outcasts of Israel have for thousands of years been scattered. The voice crying in the wilderness has a special appropriation to these [Indian] Hebrews. As it had a kind of literal fulfillment in the preaching of [Isaiah] the forerunner of John [the Baptist], for a short time in the wilderness of Judea;

so it is to have a kind of literal fulfillment, upon a much greater scale, in the missions which shall recover the ten tribes from the vast wilderness of America.

The restoration-recovery involved self-awareness of the ancient Israelite legacy, conversion to Christ, and return. Like Crawford and Boudinot, Smith said that teachers were needed to explain their unconscious legacy—the early blessings, the ejection from their ancient Land. The Indians should be told that the end of time was nearing when they would return to their "God of their salvation"; that the "Great Spirit above the clouds" was about to call them "to come and receive His grace by Christ, the true star from Jacob, the Shiloh who has come (Genesis 49:10), to whom the people must be gathered." Christians would be delivering the Indians from "a mystical wilderness of spiritual wretchedness, of ignorance and moral death," and from the "literal wilderness" of America into the Land of Israel. He called upon fellow American Christians to commit themselves to the endeavor:

> If our natives be indeed from the tribes of Israel, American Christians may well feel that one great object of their inheritance here [in America] is that they may have a primary agency in restoring those 'lost sheep of the house of Israel' [Matthew 10:6]. Those Hebrews first occupied the blessings of the covenant and the old and dark dispensation. Then the Christian gentiles came into possession of the blessings of this covenant, under its last, the Christian dispensation. Noah, more than four thousand years ago, in prophetic rhapsody, uttered the following prediction: 'God shall enlarge Japheth (i.e., the gentiles); and He shall dwell in the tents of Shem' (or of the Hebrews) [Genesis 9:27]. But this event is only until the fulness of the gentiles be come in [Romans 11:25]; then shall the Hebrews again take their place as God's first born [Jeremiah 31]. Let us then be active in restoring their long lost blessing.

Smith emphasized that the restoration was literal. The prophetic "eye" rested "on a literal restoration of his long lost brethren" to Zion.[38]

Upon their respective returns to the Land of Israel, the descendants of Judah and Benjamin and the Ten Lost Tribes would re-unify under Christ. Smith cited Ezekiel's "two sticks." One was inscribed for the Jews who returned from Babylon, another for the ten tribes of Israel who revolted in the days of Rehoboam and were separated off (Ezekiel 37).

These two sticks, miraculously, become one in the prophet's mind. And this miracle, God explains [in terms of] the two nations, the Jews and Israel, becoming permanently *united* in one nation, in the Land of their fathers, and remaining holy and happy thenceforward under the reign of Christ, their spiritual David.[39]

Smith added that the converted Jews would be the most powerful force for converting the rest of the world (Zechariah 8:23), after the fall of Antichrist:

The converted Jews, taking a pre-eminent stand in the church of Christ, might be expected to burn with a holy zeal, to promote that cause of their Messiah, which they have so long trampled under foot. And beholding the millions, through the earth, dead in paganism, they would greatly desire their conversion, and make every arrangement to effect it.[40]

Smith, like Eliot and Boudinot, believed that America had a special role in the *eschaton*. American Christians, as cited above, inherited the "great object" of helping to restore the Indians. Further, the land of America would itself become transformed:

As the wilderness of Judea in a small degree blossomed as a rose when John the Baptist performed his ministry in it [Mark 1:4]; so the wilderness [Isaiah 35:1] and solitary place of *our vast continent* containing the lost tribes of the house of Israel will, on a most enlarged scale, rejoice and blossom as the rose, when the long lost tribes shall be found there and shall be gathered into Zion.[41]

For Smith, then, there was also a tripartate relationship: Christian kingdom, return-conversion of Judah and Benjamin; self-awareness-return-conversion of the Ten Lost Tribes. The crucifixion-conversion correlation was so intense for him that he expected the crucifiers to become the greatest missionaries in introducing the millennium. America loomed large in Smith's eschatology. It was God's appointed reservation for the Ten Lost Tribes in anticipation of the Christian kingdom; American Christians were especially responsible for conversion, and the land itself recalled the Holy Land of Isaiah and John the Baptist.

BARBARA A. SIMON

Little is known about Simon, a New Yorker. Her focus was not in terms of the apocalypse, which for Eliot, Crawford, Boudinot and Smith loomed atop history and defined the role of Israel and the Ten Lost Tribes-American Indian, but on conversion itself.

In her 1823 *Evangelical Review of Modern Genius,* dedicated to the American Society for Meliorating the Condition of the Jews, she carried forward the cause-effect relation of Boudinot and Smith between "unbelief in the divine character of the word made flesh" (John 1:14) and the destruction of Jerusalem and exile of Jerusalem's "family." For eighteen centuries, she explained, Israel's unbelief made the people into "a monument bearing to every nation under heaven an unwilling testimony to the truth of the *divinity* of their rejected Messiah." Simon believed that if the Jews would look upon the one they pierced and mourn for Him (Zechariah 12:10), they would be "reunited to their own olive" (Romans 11:24). The Jews once "shone like the stars of their race." Because of unbelief they became scattered and "long trodden in dust-like disgrace," but Christian faith would revive them. Like Crawford a Christian poet, she put it this way: "Nor shall thou arise, or thy tribes be restored / Till *this* which hath pierced Him, [becomes] *faith in the Lord.*"[42] In 1836 she added:

> It was by His bodily restoration to renewed life that the promises to the fathers became confirmed, His reanimated body being the earnest and pledge of those of His redeemed. Hence His *rejection* in His office of prophet by that *remnant* of the two tribes [of Judah and Benjamin] which remained after the building of the second Temple), constituted Him [as] the atonement for the whole [world].[43]

But ultimately there would be "one fold and one shepherd" (John 10:16). As Ezekiel described in his "future history," the children of Israel would be gathered from the nations into their own Land, they would become one nation in the Land, with one king. They would be redeemed from their sin and purified (Ezekiel 37).

Drawing upon Menasseh ben Israel, Edward King and (the derivative) Boudinot, she concluded that American Indians were the descendants of the Ten Lost Tribes, Isaiah's "outcasts of Israel" and "dispersed of Judah" (Isaiah 11:12).[44] In 1836 she mourned the loss of "twenty once-powerful nations which animated the extensive territory of New England":

The chiefs have gone to their early grave
Like gleams
    of a lurid day,
And like the crest of the tossing wave
Like the rush of the blast in the
    mountain cave
Like the groans of the murdered with
    none to save
Their people have passed away.

She blamed the Indians' demise in part on the Puritans (perhaps including Eliot himself?). Victims of intolerance at home they became intolerant abroad. The so-called "spiritual Israel" never questioned their usurpation of the rights of others. They presumed that what they regarded as "idolatrous practices" justified extermination. They believed they were "martyrs for the faith" with the "warrant" to root out the "Canaanites" in their "New Canaan," "that those who [were] not a people might make room for those who [were] a people."[45] But Simon also hoped that the Indians would be revived and "united in love to the redeemer." The Indians had a "secret, but heaven-whispered story":

Long have you wandered as outcasts forsaken
Been driven by the lawless to ocean's
    wild shore;
But now shall your springtime of
    promise awaken,
As vines yield their blossoms when
    winter is o'er . . .
Illumin'd by truth, that pure light of the holy!
How bright its reflection shall lighten
    from you.
O say not salvation to you hath
    moved slowly—
"The last" it o'ertakes "shall be first" [Matthew 19:30]
    to pursue.[46]

Simon did not belong to the millennialist school of the others cited here, but she did expect history to resolve itself in Christ. She shared the Ten Lost Tribe-American Indian connection and anticipated Indian conversion to Christianity and, by implication, return with all Jews to the Land of Israel. Her reference to the Puritans was ironical: Those who searched for the new Zion persecuted the authentic descendants of that Land.

CONCLUSION

What can be drawn from this material? First, considering the long period under consideration, there is a striking consistency of themes: The Ten Lost Tribes which left the ancient Holy Land in 772 B.C.E. ended up in America, where the ground was prepared for them by the "proto" Hebrews of Peleg's days. These Jews were not involved in the crucifixion and thus innocent; indeed—perhaps to contrast them with the people of Judah and Benjamin—they were under God's special protection. The discovery of the Ten Lost Tribes belonged to the apocalyptic reality detailed in Daniel and Revelation—they were identified specifically in Revelation. Once discovered they would be educated about their Hebrew origin and legacy and then converted. Here, to the Christian mind, were the Jews who did not err and oppose Christ; the ones who evidenced Christ's truth and His reality in mankind. Once converted they would return with the rest of newly converted Jews elsewhere in the world to the Land of Israel under Christ. America had a crucial role in this transformation. It was "raised up" to provide a refuge for Jews who would remain pure for Christ. Here the Christian *eschaton* would begin—as testified to in Scriptural references to the East, and as testimony to the innocent American Indian who would come to Christ without ever having betrayed Him. Meanwhile, both the Church of Rome (a later version of the Jewish Antichrist) and inherently perverse Islam which occupied Christ's Land, would be destroyed.

For our thinkers, the Ten Lost Tribes-American Indian connection was a theological necessity. This necessity overwhelmed the lack of historical proof and allowed satisfaction with Scriptural text and apparent similarities in belief, ritual and customs. The apocalypse required Ten Lost Tribes and our Christians were going to provide them. They dedicated themselves to making the discovery and validating it through missionary work—which in turn would reinforce the connection and fulfill the authors' own pre-eschatological roles.

NOTES

1. The earliest exposition appears to have been Johannes F. Lumnius, *De extremo dei Judicio et Indorum vocatione* 2 (Venice: Apud Dominicum de Farris, 1569).

2. With regard to the Catholics, see John L. Phelan, *The Millennial Kingdom of the Franciscans in the New World,* second edition (Berkeley: University of California, 1970), 24-26. Here Phelan writes: "The popularity of the Jewish-Indian myth in the New World was due partly to the fact that it provided a kind of explanation for the origin of American man. But I suggest that the real source of appeal for the spread of this curious legend can be found only in the apocalyptical mood of the Age of Discovery. If the Indians were in reality the lost tribes, such a discovery would be convincing evidence that the world was soon to end." Phelan cites the Spanish American Gregorio Garcia, *Origen de los Indios de el Nuevo Mundo* (Valencia: En casa de P.P. Mey, 1607). Leonard I. Sweet, "Christopher Columbus and the Millennial Vision of the New World," *The Catholic Historical Review* 72 no. 3 (July 1986): 369-382. On Mormons, see Book of Mormon. *Nephi* 1, 2 and 3. On Jews, see Mordecai M. Noah, *Discourse on the Evidence of the American Indians Being the Descendants of the Lost Tribes of Israel.* Delivered before the Mercantile Library Association, Clinton Hall (New York: Jay Van Norden, 1837).

3. The text connecting the appearance of the lost tribes and the apocalypse is in Revelation: "And I heard the number of them which were sealed. And there were sealed an hundred and forty and four thousand of all the tribes of the children of Israel. Of the tribe of Judah were sealed twelve thousand. Of the tribe of Reuben were sealed twelve thousand. Of the tribe of Gad were sealed twelve thousand. Of the tribe of Asher were sealed twelve thousand. Of the tribe of Menasseh were sealed twelve thousand. Of the tribe of Simeon were sealed twelve thousand. Of the tribe of Levi were sealed twelve thousand. Of the tribe of Issakhar were sealed twelve thousand. Of the tribe of Zebulon were sealed twelve thousand. Of the tribe of Benjamin were sealed twelve thousand." Revelation 7:4-8.

4. Cotton Mather, *Magnalia Christi Americana. Or, the ecclesiastical history of New England from its first planting in the year 1620 unto the year of our Lord 1698 (MCA). Antiquities. The first book of the New English history. Reporting the design whereon, the manner wherein, the people whereby, the several colonies of New England were planted* (Hartford: S. Andrus, 1853), 336. Cited by Sidney H. Rooy, "John Eliot. The establishment of the mission," *The Theology of Missions in the Puritan Tradition* (Delft: W.D. Meinema, 1965), 156.

5. John Eliot, *The Christian Commonwealth. Or, the civil policy of the rising kingdom of Jesus Christ* (London: Publisher?, 1659). Cited by Rooy, 230-235.

6. Eliot, *Harmony of the Gospels* (Boston: Publisher?, 1678), 126, 79-80. Cited by Rooy, 228-230.

7. John Dury, "An Epistolical Discourse to Mr. Thorowgood Concerning His Conjecture that the Americans are Descended from the Israelites" in Thomas Thorowgood, *Jews in America. Or, probabilities that the Americans are of that race. With the removal of some contrary reasonings, and earnest desires for the effectual endeavors to make them Christian* (London: Printed by W.H., 1650), 23-43. Thorowgood included correspondence between Dury and Menasseh ben Israel. Cf. Menasseh ben Joseph ben Israel. *The Hope of Israel (Mikve Israel). . . . In this treatise it is showed the place wherein the ten tribes at this present are proved partly by the strange relation of one Anthony Montezinus [Aaron Levi], a Jew, of what befell him as he travelled over the mountains Cordillaere, with divers other particulars about the restoration of the Jews* (London: 1650). Thorowgood, *Jews in America. Or, probabilities that those Indians are Judaical. Made more probable by some additionals to the former conjectures. An accurate discourse is premised of Mr. John Eliot (who first preached the gospel to the natives in their own language) touching their origination and his vindication of the planters* (London: printed for H. Brome, 1660). The Puritan Richard Baxter (1615-1691) differed: "As to the doctrine of the Jews' conversion, I have told you somewhat of the reason of my dissent. I am past doubt that the ten tribes were sent back with the rest, that (though mixed with corruption) the Romans found them there, and that almost all the infidel Jews were killed by Tiberius, Trojan and Adrian, and the scattered Jews are but the progeny of the nation left, and had the liberty of their country." Richard Baxter to Increase Mather, cited by Rooy, 234n.

8. Eliot drew from Broughton (1549-1612) for tracing the Ten Lost Tribes eastward into America: "It seemeth to me probable that these [Indian] people are Hebrews, of Ever, whose sons the Scripture [source?] sends farthest east (as it seems to me) and learned Broughton put some of them over into America, and certainly this country was peopled eastward from the place of the ark's resting, seeing the finding of them by the west is but of yesterday." See Hugh Broughton, *A Consent of Scripture* (London: Publisher?, 1620).

9. Eliot, *The Day-Breaking. If not the sun-rising of the gospel with the Indians in New England* (London: Printed by R. Cotes, 1647), 15-16. Cited by Rooy, 183.

10. Eliot, "[Letter to Mr. Edward Winslow (1595-1655) of 8 May 1649]," *The Light Appearing More and More Towards the Perfect Day. Or, a farther discovery of the present state of the Indians in New England concerning the gospel among them* (London: 1651), 14-18. Eliot, "The Learned Conjectures of Rev. Mr. John Eliot Touching the Americans, of New and Notable Consideration. Written to Mr. Thorowgood," in Thorowgood, *Jews in America,* (1650), 1-22. Cf. Edward Winslow, *The Glorious Progress of the Gospel, Amongst the Indians in New England* (London: Printed for Hannah Allen, 1649).

11.. See Charles Crawford, *The Christian. A poem in six books,* second edition (Philadelphia: Printed by Benjamin Johnson, 1794). *Idem, A Dissertation on the "Phaedon" of Plato. Or, dialogue of the immortality of the* soul. With some general observations about the writings of that philosopher. To which is annexed a psychology. Or, an abstract investigation of the nature of the soul in which the opinions of all the celebrated metaphysicians on the subject are discussed (London: Printed for the Author, 1773). On Crawford see Lewis Leary, "Charles Crawford. A forgotten poet of early Pennsylvania," Pennsylvania Magazine of History and Biography 83 (July 1959): 293-306.

12. Pierre Charlevoix, Journal of a Voyage to North America. Undertaken by order of the French King. Containing the geographical description and natural history of that country, particularly Canada. Together with an account of the customs, characters, religion, manners and traditions of the original inhabitants, 2 volumes (London: Printed for R. and J. Dodsley, 1761).

13. William Bartram, Travels Through North and South Carolina, Georgia, East and West Florida. The Cherokee country, the extensive territories of the Muscogulges or Creek confederacy, and the country of the Choctaws. Containing an account of the soil and natural productions of those regions, together with observations on the manners of the Indians (Philadelphia: Printed by James and Johnson, 1791).

14. [William] Penn, "A Letter from William Penn, Proprietor and Governor of Pennsylvania in America, to the Committee of the Free Society of Traders to that Province Residing in London. Containing a general description of the said province, its soil, air, water, seasons and produce, both natural and artificial, and the good increase thereof. With an account of the natives, or aborigines [16 August 1683]," A Collection of the Works of William Penn 2 (London: Publisher?, 1726): 699-706.

15. Jonathan Edwards, Observations on the Language of the [Mohegan] Indians. In which the extent of that language in North America is shown; its genius is grammatically traced; some of its peculiarities and some instance of analogy between that and the Hebrew are pointed out (New Haven: Printed by Josiah Meigs, 1758).

16. Charles Beatty, The Journal of a Two Month's Tour. With a view of promoting religion among the frontier inhabitants of Pennsylvania. And of introducing Christianity among the Indians to the westward of the Alleghany mountains. To which are added remarks on the language and custom of some particular tribes among the Indians. With a brief account of the various attempts that have been made to civilize and convert them, from the first settlement of New England to this day (London: Printed for W. Darenhill, 1768).

17. James Adair, The History of the American Indians. Particularly those nations adjoining to the Mississippi, east and west Florida, Georgia, South and North Carolina, and Virginia. Containing an account of their origin, language, manners, religious and civil customs, laws, form of government, punishments, conduct in war and domestic life, their habits, diet, agriculture, manufactures, diseases and method of cure. . . . (London: Printed for E. and C. Dilly, 1775).

18. Crawford cited Thomas Salmon, *A New Geographical and Historical Grammar* (London: W. Johnson, 1758). Charles Crawford, *Observations Upon the Fall of Antichrist and the Concomitant Events* (Philadelphia: Publisher?, 1786). Cf. also Crawford, "Preface," *Looking Glass for the Jews by [Quaker Founder] George Fox [1624-1691]*, "in which [Crawford] contends for the unlimited toleration of the Jews," Crawford, *Observations*, 32.

19. Crawford, "Preface," *The Christian. A poem in six books*, 5-6.

20. Crawford, *Three Letters to the Hebrew Nation* (London: 1817), translated into German in Solomon Bennett, "Kritische und theologische Erwiederung auf das von Lord Crawford erschienene Sendschreiben an die hebraeische Nation," *Israel's Bestaendigkeit. Eine unbefangene Beleuchtung mehrererwichtiger Bibelstellen, insbesondere sogenannte messianische Weissagungen. In kritischer Erwiederung auf das von Lord [Carl] Crawford erschienene oeffentliche Sendschreiben an die hebraeische Nation, nebst einen kurzen Abriss der juedischen Geschichte und Nachrichten ueber den Zustand der heutigen Juden in Europe. Aus dem englischen [The Constancy of Israel, London 1809] uebersetzt* (Darmstadt: J.P. Diehl, 1835), 1-79.

21. Crawford, *Observations Upon the Fall of Antichrist and the Concomitant Events.*

22. Crawford, *An Essay Upon the Eleventh Chapter of the Revelation of St. John. In which it is shown that the words "And in the same hour was there a great earthquake, and the tenth part of the city fell, and in the earthquake were slain of men seven thousand," Revelation 11/13, relate to Jerusalem and not to Rome or France* (Philadelphia: Asbury Dickins, 1800).

23. Crawford, *An Essay Upon the Propagation of the Gospel* (Philadelphia: J. Gates, 1799). *Idem, An Essay Upon the Propagation of the Gospel. In which there are numerous facts and arguments adduced that many of the Indians in America are descended from the Ten Tribes*, second edition (Philadelphia: Printed by James Humphreys, 1801).

24. See George A. Boyd, *Elias Boudinot. Patriot and statesman 1740-1821* (Princeton, NJ: Princeton University, 1952).

25. To reinforce his point that Jews themselves were authentically committed to resurrection, Boudinot cited Talmudic and Jewish liturgical sources. Elias Boudinot, *The Second Advent. Or, the coming of the messiah in glory, shown to be a Scripture doctrine and taught by divine revelation from the beginning of the world. By an American layman* (Trenton, NJ: D. Fenton and S. Hutchinson, 1815), 3, 16-19, 36-71, 228-229, 514-515, 542-543. Boudinot, *A Star in the West. Or, a humble attempt to discover the long lost ten tribes of Israel, preparatory to their return to their beloved city, Jerusalem* (Freeport, NY: books for Libraries, 1970 edition of 1816 original), iii, 27, 43-50, 75, 87, 297.

26. Boudinot, *A Star in the West.*

27. See Edward King Viscount Kingsborough, "Arguments to Show that the Jews in Early Ages Colonized America," *Antiquities of Mexico* 6 (London: A. Aglio, 1831): 232-420; "Note 31," *Antiquities of Mexico* 8 (London: A. Aglio,

1848): 3-268.

28. Boudinot, *Second Advent*, 514-515.

29. Boudinot, *A Star in the West.*

30. Ibid.

31. Ibid.

32. Boudinot, *Second Advent.*

33. William B. Sprague, "Ethan Smith," *Annals of the American Pulpit. Or commemorative notices of distinguished American clergymen of various denominations, from the early settlement of the country to the close of the year eighteen hundred and fifty-two* 2 (New York: R. Carter and Brothers, 1857): 296-300. See David Persuitte, *Joseph Smith and the Origins of the Book of Mormon* (Jefferson, NC: McFarland, 1985), 143-147. On Smith and the Millerites see William Miller, "A Review of Ethan Smith's and David Campbell's Exposition of the Little Horn [Daniel 7/8] and Return of the Jews [15 March 1840]," *Views of the Prophecies and Prophetic Chronology. Selected from manuscripts of William Miller. With a memoir of his life by Joshua V. Himes* (Boston: M.A. Daw, 1881), 172-181. Isaac Wellcome, *History of the Second Advent Message and Mission, Doctrine and People* (Yarmouth, Maine: Publisher?, 1874), 163-169.

34. Jedidiah Morse, *A Report to the Secretary of War of the United States [John C. Calhoun] on Indian Affairs. Comprising a narrative of a tour performed in the summer of 1820, under a commission from the President of the United States, for the purpose of ascertaining for the use of the government the actual state of the Indian tribes of our country* (New Haven: Printed by S. Converse, 1822).

35. Boudinot, *Second Advent.*

36. Ethan Smith, *View of the Hebrews. Exhibiting the destruction of Jerusalem, the certain restoration of Judah and Israel, the present State of Judah and Israel, and an address of the prophet Isaiah relative to their restoration* (Poultney, Vermont: Smith and Shute, 1823), iii, 6-7, 70-71, 158-161, 167. Smith, *View of the Hebrews. Or, the Tribes of Israel in America,* second edition (Poultney, Vermont: Smith and Shute, 1825), 172, 247-250.

37. Samuel F. Jarvis, *A Discourse on the Religion of the Indian Tribes of North America* (New York: C. Wiley, 1820).

38. Smith, *View of the Hebrews.*

39. Smith, *A Dissertation on the Prophecies Relative to Antichrist and the Lost Tribes. Exhibiting the rise, character and overthrow of that terrible power. And a treatise on the seven apocalyptic vials* (Charlestown, Mass.: Printed by Samuel T. Armstrong, 1811), 207.

40. Smith, *Key to the Revelation. In thirty-six lectures, taking the whole book in course* (New York: J. and J. Harper, 1833), 381.

41. Smith, *View of the Hebrews.*

42. Barbara A. Simon, *Evangelical Review of Modern Genius. Or, truth and error contrasted* (New York: D.A. Borrenstein, 1823).

43. [Barbara A.] Simon, *The Ten Tribes of Israel. Historically identified with the aborigines of the Western Hemisphere* (London: R.B. Seeley and W. Burnside, 1836), xv-xvi.

44. Simon, *The Ten Tribes of Israel*, xxxix-xi.

45. Simon, *The Ten Tribes of Israel*, 368-370.

46. Simon, *A View of the Human Heart. A series of allegorical designs representing the human heart from its natural to its regenerated state. With explanatory addresses, meditations, prayers and hymns. For the instruction of youth* (New York: E.H. Simon, 1825).

Religious Conflicts between Sephardic and Christian Settlers in Seventeenth and Eighteenth Century North America

Yitzchak Kerem

The acculturation of the early Sephardic settlers into Christian North American Society was successful, but the process was full of obstacles. For these Marranos, or descendants of Spanish and Portuguese expulsees, the English and French-speaking populated areas of North America symbolized a future of freedom, where religious practice and communal life could flourish.

For the Jews under the short-lived Dutch rule and under later British colonial rule, religious liberties and freedom had to be attained. Jews were never denied the right to pray on American soil, but restrictions placed upon them hindered their communal growth and professional life. Once they established themselves and elevated their socio-economic status, organized Jewish religious life could develop.

Jews migrated to the Americas at a time when any faith other than the official religion was outlawed by the respective Dutch and British colonial powers. In practice, Jews could worship together, but the right to build synagogues and establish cemeteries only came about through arduous and frequent political struggles. The Sephardic settlers wanted to integrate into the general society and contribute to the national effort in the colonies, while restoring their religious heritage.

In Colonial America, the predominantly Christian society often discriminated against non-Christian political participation, but specific legislation against Jewish religious practice did not exist. Despite legislation enacted in opposition to the inclusion of Jews and other minorities during the Colonial period and even after the establishment of the United States, Jews found avenues to exert political influence, enter the political arena, and hold public office.

When the first Sephardic Jews arrived in the Dutch colony of New Amsterdam in 1654, they immediately encountered opposition from Governor Peter Stuyvesant. The group of twenty-three Jews departing from Recife, Brazil, after the Portuguese conquest of Dutch-ruled Brazil, laid the base for the future Spanish-Portuguese synagogue, Shearith Israel, built in New Amsterdam. Religious and communal rights were only granted by the Dutch in new Amsterdam after Jewish political pressure and struggle. Because the Jews couldn't pay for their trip, Stuyvesant sought to deport them, but his efforts were thwarted by Jewish perseverance and resourcefulness. Stuyvesant, as well as his predecessor, opposed Jews and any religious group other than the Dutch Reformed Church. "Influenced by a loyalty to his church, which had been fortified through the religious war between Holland and Spain, he was determined not to permit public religious worship other than that of his own church."[1] Sephardic Jews in Amsterdam covered the debt, and their influence in the Dutch West India Company, which oversaw the colonies, led to permission for the Jews to settle.[2] This set a precedent for other denominations to settle in North America, and shortly Jews were working for freedom of worship and equality in citizenship in their new land.

Even though Stuyvesant attempted to curb Jewish involvement in trade, the Dutch West India Company stood firm and promoted free enterprise. In 1665, New Amsterdam local officials and the Supreme Council judged that Jews must leave the colony. Jews in Amsterdam again intervened and the Dutch West India Company permitted settlement, trade, and travel of Portuguese Jews in New Netherlands on the condition that the poor not be a burden on the company and that they be supported by the Jewish nation.[3] At varying times, Dutch Jewish stockholders and the local Portuguese Jewish community in Amsterdam pressured the company. In 1630, a few months before the Dutch captured Brazil from the Portuguese, the council of the West India Company declared freedom of conscience in its administrative guidelines for the Dutch settlements throughout the Americas. Stuyvesant, however, had his own set of rules *vis-a-vis* Jews, and granted their rights only after firm directives from the Dutch West India Company in Holland.

In 1656, when some of their rights were denied, the Jews of New Amsterdam again appealed to the Jews of Amsterdam. Despite orders, the governor wasn't allowing Jews to practice their religion, Jews were forbidden to deal in real estate, they could not have Christian employees, and they couldn't trade freely. New Jewish immigrants needed assurance that their rights would be upheld in New Netherlands. Local officials sought to expel Jews on the grounds that a recent Judeo-Iberian emigré, Abraham de Lucena, had kept his store open during the Sunday sermon, which every citizen was expected to attend twice on that day. However this was not enough to dislocate the Jews.[4]

Jews were part of a succession of migrations, that opened up the door to freedom. According to De Sola Pool, the pressure and determined stand of the Jews "proved to be an entering wedge that reinforced the efforts of Christian denominations also for the 'free and public exercise' of their religion." Freedom came only haltingly. Lutherans beginning in 1653, Jews beginning in 1654, Quakers from 1657, and others later in that century and in the next who dangerously followed their faith, owe one another something of the freedom which all today enjoy."[5]

Jacob bar Simson and Asser Levy succeeded in attaining the right of the Jews to be involved in the self-defense of the colonies against the Indians. By 1660 they had attained the right to work, but they lacked and requested religious liberty. In anticipation that the Jews would want to construct a synagogue, the Company adopted a "let's wait and see until they actually request" approach, but limited religious worship to within the quietness of Jewish homes. Stuyvesant feared that granting freedom of worship to Jews would set a precedent to force the Company to also grant such rights to the Lutherans and the Papists.[6]

When the Jews made a petition to establish a cemetery in 1655, the response of the local burgomasters, schipens, and schout was that a separate piece of land would be granted to them when the need actually arose. The following year, when the determined Jews applied again, they succeeded in obtaining a graveyard, at an unknown site.[7]

While New Amsterdam's Dutch authorities waited for permission from Holland's Dutch West India Company to deport the Jews, fifteen Jewish families left and settled in Newport. Since the establishment of Rhode Island by Roger Williams (who had been expelled from Massachusetts because of his faith), laws had been enacted that made freedom of religious worship possible.[8] The New England pilgrim Puritan settlers, who had come to organize their lives and religion free of persecution, conducted their lives in accordance with Old Testament principles and religious rites, such as Sabbath commemoration and high priest rituals. Nonetheless, they treated Jews as strangers to the effect that: "For a long time only those who were company members, Church members, and Freemen could vote or hold office, whereas, the majority, the bondsmen, were denied such rights."[9]

The fifteen Jewish families from New Amsterdam came to Newport, which had previously established commercial relations with New Amsterdam, and felt secure in their new location. In 1658 they established their religious and social life in the home of Mordechai Campanall, where they had a prayer "minyan" and "masonry" meetings. However, in accordance with the Navigation Acts, enacted in England in 1651, 1660, and 1663, strangers, and non-citizens were not permitted to trade within the colonies, and the New England Jewish communities did not grow. In 1677 the Jews purchased their own cemetery.[10]

When the English captured New Amsterdam in 1664 and the city became New York, the struggle to obtain religious freedom continued. Whereas in the home country of England, where Sephardic Jews were being indicted for holding public worship and not attending church in the 1670s and 1680s, in the territories of Colonial America, the Jews were allowed to practice their religion as long as the peace was not upset. In 1682 in New York it was reported that Jews held separate meetings and in the same year a second cemetery was acquired. However, even in 1685 the petition of the Jews to the English Governor Dongon requesting the right to exercise their religion publicly was refused by the local council. Public worship was only tolerated for those that professed faith in Christ. Despite positive gestures like Dongon's 1686 statement permitting all to exercise their religion openly as long as the peace was not disturbed and his annulment of the restrictive city charter at the orders of the king, in 1691 the general assembly relapsed by "limiting the liberty of worship to those professing faith in God by Jesus Christ."[11] Nonetheless, in about 1686 public Jewish services were already being held and in 1695 a synagogue was reported.[12] Thus, the Jews of New York fought to create religious freedom and assisted in defining this practice. They contributed to the aggrandizement of religious liberty and helped in its attainment.

Conditions for Jews were not always favorable, and the ramifications of the precarious status of Jews often caused great inconveniences. In order to do business, Jews often needed denization privileges, which were connected to the burgher license, attained through military service which Asser Levy and Jacob ben Simson had fervently fought for in the mid-1650s.[13]

Under the Navigation Acts of 1660 and their later additions, an alien in England or the colonies needed to be "denized" or preferably "naturalized" in order to conduct business as a merchant-shipper, especially when trading in distant colonies. Some born to Jewish aliens in the colonies were as free as those born in England regarding the payment of duties and customs.[14]

One obtained citizenship through naturalization, denization, or freedom of the city. Denization was granted by the ruler or the provincial governors. It permitted one to carry on business, but it was temporary and revocable. Even though naturalization accorded more privileges than denization, it did not grant political rights which "were separately defined in the charters and provincial laws; these were frequently dependent upon landed wealth and religious affiliation."[15] "Freedom of the city" was awarded by a municipality and it provided the right to retail selling, and the practice of trade, a craft, or an occupation. Degrees of citizenship varied from colony to colony, so for the Jew voting was a right found in some colonies and not in others.

Rabbi Couty, a New York Jewish burgher, had his boat and cargo wrongly confiscated in 1671 in Jamaican waters by the decision of the Court of Admiralty there, who deemed him an alien since he was a Jew. After he appealed, the Council for Trade and Plantations determined that he was a "free citizen" due to his colonial denization rights and that he had acted lawfully in accordance with the Act of Navigation. Jacob Lucena had continual difficulties. In 1670 he was found guilty in Hartford, Connecticut court of being "notorious in his lascivious dalliance and wanton carriage and profers to several women."[16] Even though he was fined twenty Lira Sterling and was threatened with a flogging penalty if he didn't pay, when he appealed the large sum, two days later the sum was reduced by half because he was a Jew.

Unfortunately in 1678 Lucena was discriminated against when he was not permitted to send a load of goods up the Hudson to Esopus, now known as Kingston. After protesting to Edmund Andros, Governor General of the American territories, he was given the right to send his goods, but had to pay over twelve liras sterling. The freedoms for trade that the 1655 Directors of the Dutch West India Company permitted to the New York Jews in their "charter" were paradoxically denied to Lucena by the British in 1678. Furthermore, in 1685 "Rabbi" Saul Brown was prohibited from opening a retail shop because the authorities held him to the letter of the law and he had not formally been made a freeman of the town. Last, but not least, in 1737, in the midst of a controversy about a contested seat in the New York Assembly, Jews were not allowed to vote for the candidates. Previously, they had voted, but would not vote again until 1761.[17]

The Naturalization Act of 1740 enabled every Jew in the Colonies to become naturalized, but there were two noteworthy exceptions. When Newport residents Aaron Lopez and Isaac Elizar applied in 1761 to the legislature of the Rhode Island Colony, they were referred to the courts. The Superior Court of the Judicature in the County of Newport rejected thier applications claiming that in accordance with a law made and passed in 1663, "No person who does not profess the Christian Religion can be admitted free into the Colony."[18]

Thus Lopez moved to Swansey, Massachusetts, where after a two month residence, he submitted a petition for naturalization to the Bristol County Superior Court of Judicature. After showing compliance with the 1740 Act and adhering to three necessary oaths, he became naturalized in 1762. His fellow Jewish petitioner, Isaac Elizar, was naturalized a year later in New York.

Even though James Lucena had been granted naturalization only a year before Elizar and Lopez applied to the same bodies, the Rhode Island Lower House denied the application of the above two Jews on the premise that "they were Jews, declaring that no member of that religion had the right to hold any office or to vote in choosing others. The Upper House averred that foreigners in the plantations were entitled to naturalization but blandly referred them to the judges of the Superior Court."[19]

The next year the court judged that the colony was already too over-populated. Marcus pointed out that the court had regressed a century, ignoring the Act of Parliament of 1740, to rule that "by a law made and passed in the year 1663, no person who does not profess the Christian religion can be admitted free of this colony."[20]

Maryland and South Carolina were noted for their legislation infringing upon full rights for those of the Jewish faith. Maryland's famous 1649 act of toleration provided toleration, religious freedom for Roman Catholics and Protestants, but not for Jews as it was explicitly stipulated. The South Carolina State Constitution of 1776 required the chief executive of the colony to take an oath to "Maintain and defend the law by G-d, and the Protestant religion and the Liberties of America." The Sephardic Jewish member of the Provisional Congresses of 1775 and 1776, Francis Salvador, saw no reason to record his objection to this provision. Although the law was aimed against the Catholics, the Jews found no reason to be concerned.[21]

Salvador was an exception as a Jewish politician. The South Carolina election law of 1721 excluded the Jews since it only enabled "every free white man . . . professing the Christian religion" to vote, and each candidate elected to the assembly had to give an oath "on the holy evangelists," which no Jew could take.[22] In 1697 Simon Valentine applied for alien rights and at the beginning of the eighteenth century four Charleston Jews were reported to have been naturalized by the British as aliens of the Jewish nation. Reznikoff described the general situation of Jewish rights in the following manner:

> The Jews of Charles Town were allowed to live openly as Jews and in fact to have a house of worship, in spite of the fact by law, unrestricted freedom was the right of Protestants only; Jews might be naturalized; trade, own property, including land and slaves, and leave their property by will; appear as witnesses by taking an oath on the Pentateuch; and they had merely to look at other times, or other lands at that time, to think themselves fortunate.[23]

The state of religious freedom in South Carolina represented a certain dichotomy for the early Colonial American Sephardic congregation. While colonies professed an openness to religious freedom, on paper religious laws were phrased to exclude the Jews. John Locke, the English philosopher who served as architect for the constitution of the Carolina colony, made religious freedom the law of the land. "No person whatsoever," he wrote, "shall disturb, molest or persecute another for his speculative opinion in religion or his way of worship." And speaking of the Jews, Locke wrote, "If we allow the Jews to have private houses and dwelling places among us, why should we not allow them to have synagogues?"[24] Thus, in this spirit, Jews were attracted to Charleston since it offered them a degree of religious and economic freedom.

However, the statutes of the Carolina colony, while enabling opportunities for wide dissent, also required that "no person above seventeen years of age shall have any benefit or protection of the law, or be capable of any profit or honor, who is not a member of some church or profession."[25] The prejudicial exclusion of non-Christians points to a state of limited toleration for Jews and reflects a bias against members of other faiths.

Even though the United States Constitution awarded equality to all of citizens in the areas of civil rights and religious privileges, some of the state constitutions did not grant the same benefits. In 1787 Maryland's constitution stipulated that only Christians could hold public offices or commissions. The Baltimore Jewish merchant, Solomon Etting, unsuccessfully petitioned the General Assembly to award all the rights of citizenship to Jews. In 1818, Thomas Kennedy from Washington County introduced a bill in the state legislature for full equality for all religious groups and removal of religious restrictions for officeholders. Only in 1823 did the legislature give its approval, but before the bill was presented to the General Assembly to be confirmed, much opposition arose throughout the state on grounds that it permitted atheists to hold public office. In the 1823 elections, Kennedy and the other supporters of the bill were not reelected. Kennedy was reelected in 1824 and he introduced a bill enabling those professing Judaism to run for public office. This bill, entitled the "Jew Bill," was accepted by the legislature and became law in 1826. In that year Solomon Etting and Jacob Cohen were both elected to the Baltimore City Council.[26]

Not many Jews went to Virginia, where the Church of England was the established church. Virginia lacked a middle-class merchant group and was primarily agricultural. Moreover, until 1784 the legislature did not permit Jews to perform marriages. Jews, of course, found such conditions unattractive and offensive, and since colonial America provided great freedom of mobility, Jews sought settlement in areas where both the religious laws and the popular perceptions governing the inhabitants proved more appealing.[27] Although the Sephardic Isaiah Isaacs was the first known Jew to settle in Richmond in 1769, not very many Jews settled there before the Revolution. There is no evidence that Jews utilized the Naturalization Act of 1740 to settle in Virginia. Earlier laws were designated to oppose all those that "failed to embrace or could not be embraced by the Anglican faith."[28] Eakin pointed out that two and a half years before the Declaration of Independence, Baptist ministers were victims of violence and jailed for "disturbing the peace" in Virginia. In other words, for "preaching the word of God as they understood it."

Jews searched for locations where they could enjoy freedom to live and worship and earn a living.[29] The religious climate in early Virginia was not as hospitable as New York, Newport, Savannah, Charleston, or Philadelphia, where Jewish communities were already established. William Penn, the Quaker who founded what became Pennsylvania, said, "I know of no religion which destroys courtesy, civility, and kindness."[30] Thus, Jews, along with Mennonites, Baptists, Sabbatarians,

Dunkers, Well-Wishers, Presbyterians, Catholics, and Lutherans, settled in Philadelphia, the City of Brotherly Love.

After the War of Independence and the Statute for Religious Freedom, Jews were attracted to Virginia. At first the Anglican Church remained the only legalized form of worship, but Virginian statesmen encouraged the promotion of religious freedom, self-determination, and equality. Thomas Jefferson's Bill for Establishing Religious Freedom encouraged religious and political freedom by creating a separation of church and state. The Bill read as follows:

> no man shall be compelled to frequent or support any religious worship, place, or ministry whatsoever, nor shall be enforced, restrained, molested, or burthened in his body or goods, nor shall otherwise suffer on account of his religious opinions or beliefs; but that all men shall be free to profess and by argument to maintain their opinion in matters of religion, and that the same shall in no wise diminish,enlarge, or affect their civil capacities.[31]

By 1790, Richmond had about one hundred Jews in twenty-nine Jewish households.[32] The city became the capital of the commonwealth in 1779, and as it developed to become a national economic center, Jewish merchants found a niche there. An additional sign of the close rapport between the Jewish population and the political establishment was evidenced when the Sephardic Jew, Uriah P. Levy, the Navy commodore, purchased and maintained Monticello for Thomas Jefferson as a note of his admiration for the latter.[33]

In Savannah, Georgia, Jews obtained religious freedom in practice, even though they were ostracized on paper and alienated politically. Test oaths effectively barred them from public office. James Oglethorpe, member of the British Parliament and founder of the Georgia Colony, however, overruled and ignored objections of the Trustees back in England, and permitted Jews to settle in Savannah. Lawyers in Charleston saw no legal constraint on their presence since the Georgia Charter only excluded "papists" and "slaves." All but eight of the original forty-two Jews who arrived in 1733 were Sephardim and they established a congregation in Savannah that same year. Oglethorpe admired Jewish physician Dr. Samuel Nunes Ribeiro, previously the chief physician in Lisbon, who prevented an epidemic on the *William and Sarah,* a boat carrying Jewish immigrants on the Savannah River, and who offered his medical services during the colony's continual plagues.[34]

In 1740-41, as the Spanish advanced northward in the war against the British (the War of Jenkin's Ear), Sephardic Jews fled to Charleston and some went further north.[35] These Sephardim, *Conversos*, who fled Portugal in the 1720s had returned to Judaism during their stay in England before they arrived in Savannah. If Savannah fell to the Spanish, these Jews risked being accused of apostasy (as former Catholics embracing Judaism), and being burned at the stake.[36]

Sephardim returned to Savannah at the end of the 1740s when the British captured Florida, but many of the Jews who had fled did not return. According to a recent estimate, the Jewish population of Savannah in 1771 was forty-nine.[37] In 1774, there were a sufficient number of Jews to make a Congregation and it was decided to meet at the house of Mordechai Sheftall.[38]

During the Revolutionary War, most Jews sided with the revolutionaries, but there were Tories. In order to compel adherence to the revolutionary cause, the Rhode Island Assembly, in June and July 1776, passed legislation requiring loyalty oaths from all suspected Tories. In Newport, the Sephardic religious leader, Isaac Touro, refused to give an oath of loyalty on the grounds that: 1) he was still a Dutch citizen, and 2) it was against his religious principles.[39] Another Tory, Myer Polock, refused to take an oath on the grounds that it was "contrary to the custom of the Jews." Isaac Hart, who with Polock was commended by Edmund Burke for being committed to the English cause, had his property seized and was expelled from Newport in 1780. When taking refuge in a Long Island fort, he was shot, bayoneted, and clubbed to death by the Continentals. A fourth Newport Jew, Moses M. Hays, the third Sephardi out of the four Jews listed from a total of seventy-seven Newport suspects, was actually a patriot. He refused to take the oath on grounds that he resented his loyalty being questioned. He demanded that his accusers face him, and noted that being a Jew "made it all the more unjust for the authorities to demand an oath of loyalty from him because these authorities were denying him the rights and opportunities of citizenship to which he was constitutionally entitled. They were demanding the responsibilities of citizenship without conferring the privilege."[40] Hays noted that "Rhode Island was not alone in this slight, but other colonial legislatures and even the Continental Congress had failed to make provision for the rights of Jews"; then he willingly signed the oath.

CONCLUSION

In the beginning generations of Colonial American life, the Sephardic and Ashkenazic Jews, regarded as one by Christian society, were allowed to practice their religion quietly. It was the actions of persistent individuals like Asser Levy of New York and Aaron Lopez of Newport, who fought for their rights as Jews, however, that won for Jews their religious as well as civil rights. Their struggle also aided other groups in attaining religious liberty. As non-Christians who refused to take Christian oaths, Jews were usually excluded from the political arena. Nonetheless, freedom of worship—unavailable in many parts of Europe, the Iberian Peninsula, the Papal States, or in Spanish- and Portuguese-ruled Latin and South America—was secured in North America.

NOTES

1. Yitzchak Kerem, "The Impact of Sephardic Migration In The Americas," *Conference Papers of the Second Bereshit Conference,* Oct. 8-10, 1992, Villanova University, Villanova, Pennsylvania (Toledo, Spain: Toledo, confradia, in press).

2. David and Tamar De Sola Pool, *An Old Faith In The New World; Portrait of Shearith Israel 1654-1954* (New York: Columbia University Press, 1955), 8-12, 14-18.

3. Ibid., 14-18.

4. Ibid., 18-20. "Grandees" like Joseph d'Acosta, (brother to excommunicated heretic Uriel Acosta), who had been president of the Amsterdam Jewish community in 1630 and was a large shareholder in the Dutch West India Company, as well as other affluent international traders like Salvador d'Andrade and Jacob Cohen Henriques (a member of the governing board of the congregation in Recife in 1651-52), enabled the Sephardim to lay a strong base in New Amsterdam, which contributed to Jews establishing themselves and planting roots in the colony. See also Stephen Birmingham, *The Grandees, America's Sephardic Elite* (New York: Harper & Row Publishers, 1971), 20-23.

5. Ibid., 28.

6. Ibid., 22-28.

7. David de Sola Pool, *Portraits Etched In Stone; Early Jewish Settlers, 1682-1831* (New York: Columbia University Press, 1952), 7-9.

8. Samuel Broches, *Jews in New England,* vol. 1 of *Historical Study On The Jews In Massachusetts 1650-1750* (New York: Bloch Publishing Co., 1942), 5.

9. Ibid., 6.

10. Ibid., 12.

11. De Sola Pool, *An Old Faith*, 32-35; and Kerem, op.cit.

12. "Jews in Colonial America," American Jewish Historical Society, 2 (Waltham, Mass.: American Jewish Historical Society, n.d.). Jacob Rader Marcus noted that the 1695 synagogue was located on Beaver Street. See Jacob Rader Marcus, *Early American Jewry, The Jews of New York, New England and Canada 1649-1794* 1 (Philadelphia: The Jewish Publication Society of America, 1951): 48.

13. De Sola Pool, *An Old Faith*, 22-28.

14. Marcus, 38-40.

15. Ibid., 39.

16. Ibid., 35-42, 48-50.

17. Ibid., 25-27, 36-38, 41.

18. "Jews in Colonial America," 8-9.

19. Marcus, 128.

20. Ibid.

21. *Since 1749, The Story of K.K. Beth Elohim of Charleston, South Carolina* (Charleston, 1991), 2; Deborah Pessin, *History of the Jews In America* (New York and London: Abelard-Schuman, 1957), 47.

22. Charles Reznikoff, *The Jews of Charleston, A History of an American Jewish Community* (Philadelphia: The Jewish Publication Society of America, 1950), 6-7.

23. Ibid.

24. Pessin, 59-60.

25. Jacob S. Raisin, "K.K. Beth Elohim, The Cradle of Reform Judaism," *Sesquincentennial Booklet, 1824-1974, K.K. Beth Elohim, Charleston, S.C., November 22-24, 1974* (Charleston: K.K. Beth Elohim, 1974), 23-24.

26. "Jews in Colonial America," 9-10.

27. Pessin, 47.

28. Ibid., 56.

29. Frank E. Eakin Jr., *Richmond Jewry: Fulfilling The Promise* (Charleston: Congregation Beth Ahabah Museum & Archives Trust, 1986), 2-3.

30. Ibid., 3.

31. Ibid., 4.

32. Myron Berman, *Richmond Jewry, 1769-1976* (Charlottsville: The University Press of Virginia, 1979), 29-30.

33. For background about Levy see Uriah P. Levy, *Rules and Regulations for Men-of-War* (1862), and *Manual of Internal Rules and Regulations for Men-of-War* (New York: D. Van Nostrand, 1861).

34. Malcolm Stern, "The Sheftall Diaries: Vital Records of Savannah Jewry (1733-1808)," *American Jewish Historical Quarterly* 54: 246-7; and "New Light on the Jewish Settlement of Savannah," in *The Jewish*

Experience in America 1 (New York,: KTAV, 1969): 174-179.

35. B.H. Levy, *A Short History of Congregation Mickve Israel of Savannah* (Savannah: Congregation Mickve Israel, n.d.), 1-7; Rabbi Arnold Mark Belzer, interview, Savannah, Georgia, May 5, 1991; Rabbi Saul Jacob Rubin, *Third To None, The Saga of Savannah Jewry 1733-1983* (Savannah: Congregation Mickve Israel, 1983), 7.

36. Levy, 3.

37. "Jews in Colonial America," 5.

38. Stern, "The Sheftall Diaries," 250-251. For additional details on Sephardim in colonial Savannah see Pessin, 61-64; and John McKay Sheftall, "The Sheftalls of Savannah: Colonial Leaders and Founding Fathers of Georgia Judaism," in Samuel Proctor and Louis Shmier with Malcolm Stern, *Jews of the South: selected essays from the South Jewish Historical Society* (Macon, Georgia: Mercer University Press, 1984), 65-78.

39. Marcus, 154-157.

40. Ibid., 156.